bread

bread

simple recipes for delicious food every day

RYLAND PETERS & SMALL
LONDON • NEW YORK

Designer Paul Stradling

Editor Kate Eddison

Production Controller Sarah Kulasek-Boyd

Art Director Leslie Harrington

Editorial Director Julia Charles

Publisher Cindy Richards

Indexer Diana LeCore

First published in 2014 by
Ryland Peters & Small
20–21 Jockey's Fields
London WC1R 4BW
and
519 Broadway, 5th Floor
New York NY 10012

www.rylandpeters.com

Text © Valerie Aikman-Smith, Maxine Clark,
Chloe Coker, Linda Collister, Ross Dobson,
Tori Finch, Liz Franklin, Brian Glover, Dunja
Gulin, Emmanuel Hadjiandreou, Jane Mason,
Hannah Miles, Miisa Mink, Jane Montgomery
and Ryland Peters & Small 2014

Design and photographs
© Ryland Peters & Small 2014

ISBN: 978-1-84975-572-6

10 9 8 7 6 5 4 3 2 1

A CIP record for this book is available
from the British Library.

US Library of Congress Cataloging-in-
Publication data has been applied for.

Printed and bound in China

notes

- Both British (Metric) and American (Imperial plus US cups) are included in these recipes for your convenience, however it is important to work with one set of measurements and not alternate between the two within a recipe.

- All spoon measurements are level, unless otherwise specified.

- All herbs used in these recipes are fresh, unless otherwise specified.

- All eggs are medium (UK) or large (US), unless specified as large, in which case US extra-large should be used.

- When a recipe calls for the grated zest of citrus fruit, buy unwaxed fruit and wash well before using. If you can only find treated fruit, scrub well in warm soapy water before using.

- Ovens should be preheated to the specified temperatures. We recommend using an oven thermometer. If using a fan-assisted oven, adjust temperatures according to the manufacturer's instructions.

contents

introduction

Bread is one of the world's oldest prepared foods, and has been a staple for humans around the world for thousands of years. Today we are spoilt for choice when it comes to bread, with corn, rye, barley, buckwheat and many other options alongside traditional wheat recipes. Various flours and yeasts are now readily available at supermarkets, so it has never been easier to try your hand at bread-making.

The simplest loaves need only flour and water; yeast will make the dough rise and salt will bring out the flavour. With only these four inexpensive ingredients, you have a whole host of recipes at your fingertips. Once you've mastered the basic techniques, you can experiment with different grains and try various flavourings, such as herbs, spices, fruits, vegetables, nuts and seeds. Try your hand at age-old classics from around the globe, such as baguettes, ciabatta, rye, sourdough, soda bread, bagels, grissini, pita bread, naan, focaccia, pizza, flatbreads or crispbreads, and you'll be amazed at the results. You can even make sweet yeast breads and pastries such as croissants, stollen, monkey bread and maple syrup buns.

This book demystifies the science behind bread-making and makes impressive loaves accessible to the home cook. From mixing and kneading to proving and shaping, the instructions are easy to follow throughout. There is something for every occasion, and there are also a few recipes for quick breads that do not require any yeast at all, perfect for when time is short.

flour and yeast

Bread, at its most basic level, is made from flour, water, salt and yeast. All bread recipes contain some sort of flour, but some recipes, such a sourdoughs, don't use yeast to rise. Most recipes also contain salt, but this is simply to make it taste better, and whether you use the finest sea salt or ordinary table salt is up to you. The water can be substituted by an endless list of liquids, which range from milk to cider, and there are limitless possibilities when it comes to additional flavourings. The most important ingredients to understand are flour and yeast, and there are various options to choose from.

Flour

Although you can make bread out of any type of flour, you will certainly get better results with some types than others. Most types of flour contain gluten, which is what gives bread its texture. Some people have a gluten intolerance, called coeliac/celiac disease, which can have very severe symptoms. There are a few gluten-free recipes in this book. Wheat flour is the most common type of flour used in bread-making around the world, and there are various types.

Strong/bread flour has a high gluten content, which makes it a good choice for bread-making. It creates a stretchy dough that rises well.

Plain/all-purpose flour tends to be used for cakes, but it is also put to use in some bread recipes. It doesn't rise as much as strong bread flour, and produces a softer texture. It is used in some recipes in this book, but tends to be used alongside baking powder rather than yeast.

Wholemeal/whole-wheat flour is made from the whole-wheat grain, and therefore creates a heavier dough and denser loaf than white flour. It is more nutritious than white flour, and is sometimes combined with white strong/bread flour to create a lighter loaf while retaining a nutty wholegrain taste.

Rye flour contains less gluten than wheat flour, so loaves made completely with rye flour do not rise very much and have a dense texture. Rye loaves have a delicious flavour, and they work well with strong tastes, such as smoked salmon. Rye flour can be mixed with white strong/bread flour for a lovely balance of taste and texture.

Yeast

There are 3 types of yeast available: fresh, dried/active dry or instant easy-blend/rapid-rise. No matter which type you use, remember that yeast is a living micro-organism, and it needs moisture to develop.

Fresh yeast comes in beige cakes, and must be stored in the refrigerator. It can be difficult to get hold of, and it doesn't last very long. Use it before the 'use-by' date.

Dried yeast, also known as active dry yeast, is 100% yeast and it looks like little pellets. It lasts much longer than fresh yeast, but it needs to be dissolved in water before being added to the flour.

Instant yeast, also known as easy-blend or rapid-rise yeast, looks like a fine powder. It has a long shelf life, and is often sold in individual sachets. You can add it directly to the flour. Instant yeast is not 100% yeast; it also contains some additives.

Sourdough

A sourdough starter is made by capturing natural yeast in a mixture of water and flour. It takes a few days to prepare, but the results are worth the time invested.

techniques

Kneading

Once all your ingredients are mixed in the bowl (1), scrape the dough on to a clean surface and knead for 10 minutes, or as stated in the recipe (2). There are lots of different ways to knead bread – using one hand or both hands, knuckles or palms – but the most important thing is to work the dough well and stretch the gluten. The dough will change from a sticky mixture to a silky, stretchy ball. The dough should still be slightly sticky, so don't be tempted to add more flour unless you really need to.

Rising

There are various stages of rising, which differ from loaf to loaf. Follow the instructions for each particular recipe. Typically, dough will be allowed to rise twice before being baked. The first rise takes place after the kneading process, and the dough usually doubles in bulk at this stage. This can take about 2 hours at room temperature or up to 8 hours in the refrigerator. The dough must be covered so that it does not dry out during rising. Some recipes require the dough to be 'knocked back' or 'punched down' after rising. This just means punching the dough gently with your fist to release some of the air.

Shaping

For a simple loaf, pull the dough from the bowl and place it on the floured surface. Gently flatten the dough into an oval. Fold the ends of the oval into the middle, one at a time, pressing down to deal the dough together. Once you have created a rectangular shape, you can start shaping the dough into a loaf by pulling and folding the edges into the middle, turning the dough around and repeating until you have a rectangle that will fit in your loaf tin/pan (3). Place it in the tin/pan, seam-side down. Cover and allow to rise again for 30–45 minutes, until the loaf has almost doubled in bulk.

1

2

3

Making a sourdough starter

There are yeast spores present in the air and in flour. Allowing a mixture of flour and water to ferment creates a 'starter' or 'chef'. The starter takes 3–5 days to develop and, when it is ready, it can be used to create bread without using yeast. You can use white strong/bread flour, wholemeal/whole-wheat flour or rye flour, depending on the type of bread you plan on baking.

Day 1

Mix 1 teaspoon flour and 2 teaspoons water in a clear jar. Seal the jar and allow to stand overnight.

Days 2, 3, 4 and 5

Add 1 teaspoon flour and 2 teaspoons water to the jar and stir. Bubbles should appear on the surface, and more bubbles should appear each day.

Using your starter

In a large bowl, mix 1 tablespoon from the jar with 150 g/1 generous cup flour and 150 ml/⅔ cup warm water. Cover and leave to stand overnight. The next day, use the amount of starter specified in your recipe. Add 1 teaspoon flour to the remaining mixture in the jar, then seal and store in the refrigerator until you need it again.

Storing your starter

If your starter is left in the refrigerator for a long time, it can become dormant. Discard any acidic liquid from the surface, stir in 2 tablespoons flour and 2 tablespoons water, mix to a paste, seal and leave to stand overnight. If bubbles have formed the next day, it is ready to use as above. If not, repeat the process above. It can be kept indefinitely, if looked after well.

From a simple white loaf to wholesome four-flour bread, this chapter is packed with family favourites that are perfect for slicing. It includes soda breads and sourdoughs, as well as a couple of gluten-free classics too. Sandwiches will never be boring again!

everyday loaves

simple white bread

This is the recipe to start you on your bread-making adventure. You can use wholemeal/whole-wheat flour instead of white flour, if you like, but use 230 ml/scant 1 cup water instead.

300 g/2½ cups white strong/bread flour

1 teaspoon salt

3 g/⅔ teaspoon fresh yeast or 2 g/¾ teaspoon dried/active dry yeast

200 ml/¾ cup warm water

500-g/1-lb/6 x 4-in. loaf tin/pan, greased with vegetable oil

Makes 1 medium loaf

In one mixing bowl, mix the flour and salt together. This is the dry mixture. In another mixing bowl, mix the yeast and water, and stir until the yeast has dissolved. This is the wet mixture. Add the dry mixture to the wet mixture. Mix with a wooden spoon and then your hands to form a dough.

Turn the dough out onto a floured surface. Knead for 10 minutes, until the dough is smooth and elastic. Place the dough back in the bowl, cover and leave for about 1 hour, or until doubled in volume.

Turn the dough out onto a floured surface, and punch it down gently, to release the air. Flatten the dough into an oval. Fold the right end of the oval over into the middle. Now fold the left end of the oval over to the middle. Press down slightly to seal the dough together. You will now have a roughly rectangular shape. Pull and fold the top of the rectangle one third of the way toward the middle, pressing it into the dough. Swivel the dough and repeat until you have a neat loaf shape the size of your loaf tin/pan.

Place the dough into the prepared tin/pan, seam-side down. Cover and leave to rise for 30–45 minutes, or until almost doubled in size.

Preheat the oven to 240°C (475°F) Gas 9. Place a roasting pan at the bottom of the oven. Fill a cup with water and set aside.

Place the loaf in the preheated oven, pour the cupful of water into the hot roasting pan to form steam and lower the oven temperature to 200°C (400°F) Gas 6. Bake for 35 minutes, or until golden brown. Tap the bottom of the loaf – if it sounds hollow, it is done. Set the loaf on a wire rack to cool.

175g/1½ cups plain/all-purpose white flour

175g/1½ cup wholemeal/whole-wheat flour

1 teaspoon salt

1 teaspoon bicarbonate of soda/baking soda

50 g/½ cup porridge/rolled oats

50 g/3½ tablespoons butter

285 ml/1¼ cups buttermilk

a handful of mixed seeds and flour, for topping

Makes 1 loaf

Soda bread is quick and simple to make, and a welcome treat served as an accompaniment to homemade soup. It can be ready in as little as 30 minutes and makes your kitchen smell wonderful, which is a bonus!

simple soda bread

Preheat the oven to 200°C (400°F) Gas 6.

Sift the flours into a bowl and add the salt, bicarbonate of soda/baking soda and oats. Stir the dry ingredients until they are well combined.

Melt the butter and add it to the buttermilk. Make a well in the centre of the dry ingredients. Pour in the buttermilk and butter mixture, and stir with a wooden spoon until all of the dry ingredients are fully incorporated. Bring the dough together with your hands, then turn it out onto a floured work surface.

Knead the dough for 1–2 minutes and then use your hands to form it into a round on a baking sheet. Cut a deep cross in the top with a sharp knife, then sprinkle the top with some mixed seeds and flour.

Bake in the top of the preheated oven for 20–25 minutes, until the loaf is well risen and golden. Tap the bottom of the loaf – if it sounds hollow, it is done. Set the loaf on a wire rack to cool.

Soda bread is traditionally from Ireland and is very quick and easy to prepare. It contains no yeast as the recipe uses bicarbonate of soda/baking soda to make it rise. This gluten-free version uses a mixture of gluten-free brown bread flour and oat flour to give a good texture and flavour.

gluten-free soda bread

Preheat the oven to 180°C (350°F) Gas 4.

Put the flours in a large mixing bowl, and add the bicarbonate of soda/baking soda and the salt. Add the buttermilk and milk, and mix together with a wooden spoon and then your hands to form a soft dough. If it is too sticky, add a little more flour but don't overwork the dough – as there is no yeast, you need to keep the mixture as light as possible.

Form the dough into a round mound, about 4 cm/1½ in. high and 20 cm/8 in. in diameter. Cut a cross on the top of the loaf with a sharp knife and dust the top with a little extra flour. Put the loaf on the prepared baking sheet and bake in the preheated oven for 45–55 minutes, or until the bread is crusty on top. Tap the bottom of the loaf – if it sounds hollow, it is done. Set the loaf on a wire rack to cool.

The bread is best eaten on the day you make it, but can be reheated in the oven the following day.

350 g/3 cups gluten-free brown strong/bread flour, plus extra for dusting

200 g/1⅔ cups oat flour*

1 teaspoon bicarbonate of soda/baking soda

1 teaspoon salt

500 ml/2 cups buttermilk

80 ml/⅓ cup milk

baking sheet, greased

Makes 1 loaf

*Oat flour is available in health food shops and online, but if you cannot find it, substitute gluten-free plain/all-purpose flour instead.

dark rye bread

This is 100% dark rye bread, making it really dense and flavoursome. Make a sourdough starter a few days in advance, using rye flour in your sourdough starter.

150 g/1¼ cups dark rye/ pumpernickel flour

100 g/scant ½ cup rye sourdough starter (see page 11)

200 ml/¾ cup plus 1 tablespoon cold water

200 g/1⅔ cups dark rye/ pumpernickel flour

1 teaspoon salt

150 ml/⅔ cup hot water

500-g/1-lb/6 x 4-in. loaf tin/pan, greased with vegetable oil

Makes 1 medium loaf

In one mixing bowl, mix the 150 g/1¼ cups flour, sourdough starter and 200 ml/¾ cup plus 1 tablespoon cold water until well combined. Place a smaller mixing bowl upside down over it and let ferment overnight. This is the wet mixture. The next day, in another mixing bowl, mix the 200 g/1⅔ cups flour and salt together. This is the dry mixture.

Tip the dry mixture over the wet mixture, making sure you entirely cover the wet mixture with the dry. Do not mix yet. Carefully pour the 150 ml/⅔ cup hot water over the dry mixture. Quickly mix together with a wooden spoon – you don't want the hot water to have time to react with the flour.

Spoon the mixture into the prepared loaf tin/pan. Dip a plastic scraper or tablespoon in water and use to smooth the surface of the dough. Dust the loaf with flour. Cover the loaf and leave to rise for 2 hours. The bread will rise now and when it is baked, but not a huge amount, which is why a small loaf tin/pan is used for a relatively large quantity of dough.

Preheat the oven to 240°C (475°F) Gas 9. Place a roasting pan at the bottom of the oven. Fill a cup with water and set aside.

Place the loaf in the preheated oven, pour the cupful of water into the hot roasting pan and lower the oven temperature to 220°C (425°F) Gas 7. Bake the bread for 30 minutes, or until brown.

Turn the bread out of the loaf pan and set on a wire rack to cool.

This is an easy recipe for novice bakers. It was invented accidentally by Doris Grant about 60 years ago, proving that sometimes accidents taste good! It is not kneaded or shaped and has only one rising – in the tin. The Grant loaf makes great sandwiches and toast, and is excellent with soup.

the Grant loaf

700 g/5¾ cups wholemeal/
whole-wheat strong/bread flour

1 teaspoon salt

15 g/3 teaspoons fresh yeast
or a 7-g/¼-oz packet instant
easy-blend/rapid rise yeast

1 tablespoon clear honey

600 ml/2½ cups tepid water

*900-g/2-lb/8½ x 4½-in. loaf
tin/pan, greased with butter*

Makes 1 large loaf

Put the flour and salt in a large bowl and mix well with your hands.

If using fresh yeast, put the yeast in a small bowl and crumble it with your fingers. Add the honey and about one-quarter of the warm water. Mix with a teaspoon until smooth. Use your hands to make a hollow in the centre of the flour. Pour the yeast and honey liquid into the hollow, then add the rest of the water. Leave for 5 minutes – the yeast liquid will become very bubbly.

If using instant easy-blend/rapid-rise dried yeast, mix it directly into the flour, then add the honey and water.

Mix the flour into the liquid with your hands, then mix well for 1 minute, moving the dough from the sides of the bowl into the centre. Mix for a further minute, until the dough feels very slippery and elastic, and comes cleanly away from the sides of the bowl.

Lift the dough into the tin and smooth the surface with a plastic spatula. Cover loosely with a clean, damp tea towel/kitchen towel. Leave to rise for 30–40 minutes, or until the dough rises to within 1 cm/½ in. of the top of the tin. Meanwhile, preheat the oven to 200°C (400°F) Gas 6.

Bake the loaf for 35–40 minutes, or until golden brown. Tap the bottom of the loaf – if it sounds hollow, it is done. Set the loaf on a wire rack to cool.

white sourdough

This is a basic sourdough using white flour. Here it is made in a small size – this way it is just enough for a meal. If you keep you sourdough starter in the fridge, you can bake this fantastic bread on a regular basis.

250 g/2 cups white strong/ bread flour

¾ teaspoon salt

150 ml/⅔ cup warm water

75 g/⅓ cup white sourdough starter (see page 11)

proofing/dough-rising basket (500-g/1-lb capacity) or colander, lined with proofing linen or a clean tea towel/kitchen towel

baking sheet, lined with parchment paper

Makes 1 medium loaf

In one mixing bowl, mix the flour and salt together. This is the dry mixture. In another mixing bowl, weigh out the water and the sourdough starter. Stir until well combined. This is the wet mixture. Add the dry mixture to the wet mixture. Mix with a wooden spoon and then your hands to form a dough.

Turn the dough out onto a floured surface. Knead for 10 minutes, until the dough is smooth and elastic. Place the dough back in the bowl, cover and leave to rise for 1 hour.

Put the dough on a flour-dusted work surface, and shape it into a smooth, rounded disc. Dust the lined basket or colander liberally with flour and lay the dough inside it. Dust the dough with flour, and leave to rise until doubled in size – this will take 3–6 hours.

Preheat the oven to 240°C (475°F) Gas 9. Place a roasting pan at the bottom of the oven. Fill a cup with water and set aside.

Tip the dough out onto the prepared baking sheet. Gently peel away the linen or towel. Use a pair of sharp kitchen scissors to snip the surface of the bread in a circular pattern.

Place the loaf in the preheated oven, pour the cupful of water into the hot roasting pan to form steam and lower the oven temperature 220°C (425°F) Gas 7. Bake for about 30 minutes, or until golden brown. Tap the bottom of the loaf – if it sounds hollow, it is done. Set the loaf on a wire rack to cool.

This is just as simple a recipe as the White Sourdough on page 24, but to make it more wholesome, this nutritious loaf contains cracked wheat and wholemeal/whole-wheat flour to give it a lovely texture and nutty flavour.

wholegrain sourdough

400 g/3⅓ cups wholemeal/whole-wheat flour

2 teaspoons salt

160 g/⅔ cup white or wholemeal/whole-wheat sourdough starter (see page 11)

140 ml/⅔ cup warm water, plus extra if necessary

200 g/1⅓ cups cracked wheat, soaked in 200 ml/1 scant cup warm water until soft

wheatgerm and bran mixture, for coating

long proofing/dough-rising basket (900-g/2-lb capacity)

baking sheet, lined with parchment paper

Makes 1 large loaf

In one mixing bowl, mix the flour and the salt together. This is the dry mixture. In another mixing bowl, mix the sourdough starter and water together, until well combined. Stir in the soaked wheat. This is the wet mixture. Add the dry mixture to the wet mixture and mix with a wooden spoon and then your hands to form a dough. Add a little extra water if the dough is too stiff.

Turn the dough out onto a floured surface. Knead for 10 minutes, until the dough is smooth and elastic. Place the dough back in the bowl, cover and leave to rise for 1 hour.

Lightly dust a clean work surface with the wheatgerm and bran mixture. Put the dough on the work surface and roll with your hands, in the wheatgerm and bran mixture, until roughly the length and width of your proofing/dough-rising basket. Sprinkle more wheatgerm and bran inside the basket, and lay the bread inside it. Leave the dough to rise until doubled the size – this will take 3–6 hours.

Preheat the oven to 240°C (475°F) Gas 9. Place a roasting pan at the bottom of the oven. Fill a cup with water and set aside.

Tip the dough out onto the prepared baking sheet. Place the loaf in the preheated oven, pour the cupful of water into the hot roasting pan to form steam and lower the oven temperature 220°C (425°F) Gas 7. Bake for about 30 minutes, or until brown. Tap the bottom of the loaf – if it sounds hollow, it is done. Set the loaf on a wire rack to cool.

simple gluten-free loaf

This lovely loaf is both gluten-free and yeast-free, so you don't need to knead it or wait for it to rise, and it stays fresh for a couple of days. Try using beer instead of sparkling water for a 'yeasty' smell and taste.

110 g/1 cup millet flakes

350 g/2 cups millet flour

3 teaspoons baking powder

1½ teaspoons salt

450 ml/1¾ cups sparkling mineral water

1 tablespoon olive oil

2 tablespoons seeds (pumpkin, sesame, sunflower, etc.)

500-g/1-lb loaf tin/pan

Makes 1 medium loaf

Preheat the oven to 220°C (425°F) Gas 7.

Stir together the millet flakes, flour, baking powder and salt in a bowl. In a separate bowl, whisk together the sparkling water with the olive oil. Pour this into the dry ingredients, mixing vigorously with a spatula until you get a medium-thick batter.

In order to get a nicely shaped loaf, cut a sheet of parchment paper to fit inside the loaf tin/pan without any creases. Sprinkle a tablespoonful of the seeds onto the parchment, pour the dough into the tin/pan and top with the remaining seeds.

Put the tin/pan into the preheated oven, lower the temperature to 200°C (400°F) Gas 6 and bake for 1 hour, until golden.

Remove from the oven and tip the bread out of the pan, peel off the paper and allow it to cool completely on a wire rack. This will prevent the bread from absorbing moisture and will keep the crust crisp.

four-flour bread

This wholesome bread contains wholemeal/whole-wheat, rye, spelt and soya flour. It is the perfect accompaniment to a bowl of hot soup for a comforting winter lunch.

500 g/4¼ cups wholemeal/whole-wheat flour

50 g/⅓ cup rye flour

50 g/⅓ cup spelt flour

50 g/⅓ cup soya flour

2 teaspoons salt

30 g/⅓ cup porridge/rolled oats

80 g/6 tablespoons soft light brown sugar, plus 1 teaspoon

6 g/2 teaspoons dried/active dry yeast

500 ml/2 cups plus 2 tablespoons warm water

65 ml/5 tablespoons rice bran oil

900-g/2-lb/8½ x 4½-in. loaf tin/pan, greased

Makes 1 large loaf

Sift all four of the flours and salt into a large mixing bowl. Stir in any husks from the sieve/strainer, the oats and the 80 g/6 tablespoons of sugar. This is the dry mixture. Set aside.

Put the yeast and the 1 teaspoon of sugar in a small bowl and add one-quarter of the warm water. Cover and set aside for 10–15 minutes, until frothy and bubbling. This is the wet mixture.

Add the wet mixture to the dry mixture, along with the oil and remaining water. Mix together into a dough. Cover and set aside for 30–45 minutes, until risen slightly.

Turn the dough out onto a floured surface. Knead for 10 minutes, until smooth and elastic. Divide in half and form into two even balls. Sit the balls side by side in the tin/pan. Cover and set aside for 30 minutes. Preheat the oven to 220°C (425°F) Gas 7.

Lightly brush the top of the dough with water and bake in the preheated oven for 20 minutes. Reduce the oven temperature to 180°C (350°F) Gas 4 and bake for 20–25 minutes more, or until golden brown. Tap the bottom of the loaf – if it sounds hollow, it is done. Set the loaf on a wire rack to cool. This bread is best eaten on the day it is made.

beer bread

Beer has long been used all over the world to bake bread. Although now more expensive than water, in the past, beer was drunk (and in some countries is still drunk) in many cases because it was more widely available than drinking water. Whatever the history, it makes a great-tasting loaf.

250 g/2 cups wholemeal/whole-wheat flour, plus extra for dusting

50 g/⅓ cup dark or light rye flour

1.5 g/¾ teaspoon instant easy-blend/rapid-rise yeast, 3 g/1 teaspoon dried/active dry yeast, or 6 g/1⅓ teaspoons fresh yeast

220 ml/1 scant cup beer, at room temperature

1½ teaspoons salt

small proofing/dough-rising basket (500-g/1-lb capacity), well floured

baking sheet, greased

Makes 1 small loaf

If you are using instant easy-blend/rapid rise or fresh yeast, put all the ingredients in a big bowl and mix them together. Turn out onto a floured surface and knead well for 10 minutes.

If you are using dried/active dry yeast, put the flours in a big bowl and make a well. Sprinkle the yeast in the well and add half the beer. Cover and allow to rest for 15 minutes. Add the rest of the ingredients and mix. Turn out onto a floured surface and knead well for 10 minutes. The dough will be quite sticky.

Put the dough back into the bowl and cover. Allow to rest for 1–2 hours, until doubled in volume.

Turn the dough out onto an unfloured surface, and punch it down gently, to release the air. Flour your hands, shape the dough into a ball or sausage and put it in the basket. Dust the loaf with flour, cover and leave for 1 hour, or until doubled in volume.

Meanwhile, preheat the oven to 200°C (400°F) Gas 6.

Carefully turn the dough out onto the prepared baking sheet, and bake for about 45 minutes, , or until golden brown. Tap the bottom of the loaf – if it sounds hollow, it is done. Set the loaf on a wire rack to cool.

Challah is the Jewish sabbath bread and it can be made in a simple spiral shape, as described here, or plaited/braided with 4 or 6 strands (inset picture). Challah has a very delicate taste and can be eaten with either savoury or sweet food.

challah

250 g/2 cups white strong/bread flour

¾ teaspoon salt

1 tablespoon sugar

6 g/1⅓ teaspoons fresh yeast or 3 g/1 teaspoon dried/active dry yeast

80 ml/⅓ cup warm water

1 egg yolk

1 whole egg

4 teaspoons sunflower oil

1 egg, beaten with a pinch of salt, for the egg wash

poppy or sesame seeds, for sprinkling

baking sheet, lined with parchment paper

Makes 1 small loaf

In one mixing bowl, mix the flour, salt and sugar together. This is the dry mixture. In another mixing bowl, mix the yeast and water, and stir to dissolve the yeast. Beat together the egg yolk and whole egg, then add to the yeast mixture. This is the wet mixture.

Add the dry mixture to the wet mixture. Mix together with a wooden spoon and then mix in the oil until combined. Using your hands, bring it together into a dough.

Turn the dough out onto a floured surface. Knead for 10 minutes, until the dough is smooth and elastic. Place the dough back in the bowl, cover and leave for about 1 hour, or until doubled in volume.

Turn the dough out onto a floured surface, and punch it down gently, to release the air. Roll it into a long sausage with tapered ends. (Alternatively, divide the dough into 6 or 4 equal portions, roll into long sausages and plait/braid them.) Roll the dough into a tight snail shape, tucking in the ends. Place on the prepared baking sheet. Brush it all over with the egg wash, then sprinkle with poppy or sesame seeds. Cover and leave to rise for 30–45 minutes, until almost doubled in volume.

Preheat the oven to 240°C (475°F) Gas 9. Place a roasting pan at the bottom of the oven. Fill a cup with water and set aside.

Place the challah in the preheated oven, pour the cupful of water into the hot roasting pan to form steam and lower the oven temperature to 200°C (400°F) Gas 6. Bake for about 20 minutes, or until golden brown. Tap the bottom of the loaf – if it sounds hollow, it is done. Set the loaf on a wire rack to cool.

From rustic baps to delicate rolls, there is a lunchbox filler for everyone here.
Try classic white bread rolls for burgers or sandwiches, traditional bagels spread
with cream cheese, or wonderful ciabatta rolls to accompany Italian-inspired meals.

rolls

bread rolls

Bread rolls are a great alternative to sliced bread for sandwiches and they also make the best burger buns.

200 g/1⅔ cups white strong/
bread flour

¾ teaspoon salt

6 g/1⅓ teaspoons fresh yeast
or 3 g/1 teaspoon dried/active
dry yeast

130 ml/generous ½ cup
warm water

*baking sheet, lined with
parchment paper*

Makes 4 rolls

In one mixing bowl, mix the flour and salt together. This is the dry mixture. In another mixing bowl, mix the yeast and water, and stir until the yeast has dissolved. This is the wet mixture. Add the dry mixture to the wet mixture. Mix with a wooden spoon and then your hands to form a dough.

Turn the dough out onto a floured surface, and knead for 10 minutes, until the dough is smooth and elastic. Place the dough back in the bowl, cover and leave for about 1 hour, or until doubled in volume.

Turn the dough out onto a floured surface, and punch it down gently, to release the air. Divide the dough into 4 equal portions using a metal dough scraper or sharp, serrated knife.

Take one portion of dough and roll it into a round, smooth ball. Flatten one side slightly and lay it, flat-side down, on the prepared baking sheet. Repeat with the remaining dough. Cover and leave to rise for 15–20 minutes, or until almost doubled in volume.

Meanwhile, preheat the oven to 240°C (475°F) Gas 9. Place a roasting pan at the bottom of the ovent. Fill a cup with water and set aside.

Place the rolls in the preheated oven, pour the cupful of water into the hot roasting pan to form steam and lower the oven temperature to 200°C (400°F) Gas 6. Bake the rolls for about 15 minutes, or until golden brown. Tap the bottom of a roll – if it sounds hollow, it is done. Set the rolls on a wire rack to cool.

Cheese is packed with calcium, and cottage cheese is the low-fat way to have it – delicious too. Enhance these rolls with fresh herbs or dried fruit.

cottage cheese rolls

500 g/4 cups self-raising/ self-rising flour, plus extra for dusting

½ teaspoon salt

250 g/generous 1 cup cottage cheese

1 large/US extra large egg

about 150 ml/⅔ cup milk

extra milk or beaten egg, for glazing

Herb rolls

3 tablespoons chopped parsley

¼ teaspoon freshly ground black pepper

Fruit rolls

2 tablespoons golden caster/granulated sugar or 1 tablespoon clear honey

3 tablespoons dried sour cherries, cranberries or fresh blueberries

food processor

large baking sheet, floured

Makes 10 rolls

Preheat the oven to 190°C (375°F) Gas 5.

Put the flour, salt, cottage cheese and egg into a food processor and process until just mixed. With the machine running, add enough milk through the feed tube until the mixture comes together to form a soft but not sticky dough.

Turn out onto a lightly floured surface and knead lightly 2–3 times until smooth. Divide the dough into 10 equal pieces and shape each one into a ball. Arrange, spaced slightly apart, on the floured baking sheet and brush lightly with milk or egg.

Bake in the preheated oven for about 20 minutes, until golden brown and firm. Cool on a wire rack.

Best eaten while still slightly warm or within 24 hours. When thoroughly cooled, the rolls can be wrapped then frozen for up to 1 month.

Variations

Herb rolls Add the parsley and pepper to the food processor with the cottage cheese, then proceed with the recipe.

Fruit rolls Add the sugar or honey to the processor with the flour. Make the dough, as above. Knead the fruit into it, then proceed as above.

olive oil rolls

This is one of the only rustic breads of Italy that has anything other than salt, water, flour and yeast in it. Olive oil was expensive in the past, so these rolls would have traditionally been made for special occasions.

500 g/4 cups plain/all-purpose flour

2.5 g/1¼ teaspoons instant easy-blend/rapid-rise yeast, 5 g/1¾ teaspoons dried/active dry yeast, or 10 g/2 teaspoons fresh yeast

250 ml/1 cup water

75 ml/⅓ cup good-quality olive oil, plus extra to glaze

2½ teaspoons salt, plus extra to season

baking sheet, greased and lined with parchment paper

Makes 12 rolls

If you are using instant easy-blend/rapid-rise or fresh yeast, put all the ingredients in a big bowl. Mix with a wooden spoon and then your hands to form a dough.

If you are using dried/active dry yeast, put the flour in a big bowl and make a well in the middle. Sprinkle the yeast in the well and add half the water. Cover and allow to rest for 15 minutes. Add the rest of the water, the olive oil and salt. Mix with a wooden spoon and then your hands to form a dough.

Turn out onto a floured surface and knead for 10 minutes, until the dough is smooth and elastic.

Put the kneaded dough back into the bowl, cover and leave to rest for 1–2 hours, or until doubled in volume.

Turn the dough out onto an unfloured surface, and punch it down gently, to release the air. Divide the dough into 12 equal portions. Shape into tight balls and place in a ring, 1 cm/½ in. apart, on the prepared baking sheet. Cover and leave to rise for 1½ hours, or until almost doubled in size.

Meanwhile, preheat the oven to 200°C (400°F) Gas 6.

Use a pastry brush to glaze the rolls with olive oil, then sprinkle lightly with salt. Bake in the preheated oven for 30 minutes, or until golden brown. Tap the bottom of the rolls — if they sounds hollow, they are done. Set the rolls on a wire rack to cool.

Traditionally filled with cream cheese and smoked salmon, bagels now come in all sorts of flavours, both savoury and sweet. It is the boiling element of the baking process that makes them deliciously chewy.

bagels

500 g/4 cups white strong/ bread flour

3 teaspoons salt

4 teaspoons sugar

25 g/2 tablespoons unsalted or salted butter, softened and finely chopped

5 g/1 teaspoon fresh or 3 g/ 1 teaspoon dried/active dry yeast

240 ml/1 cup warm water

1 egg, lightly beaten

1 egg, beaten with a pinch of salt, for the egg wash

poppy or sesame seeds (optional)

baking sheet, greased and lined with parchment paper

Makes 9 bagels

In one mixing bowl, mix the flour, 2 teaspoons salt, the sugar and butter together. This is the dry mixture. In another mixing bowl, weigh out the yeast. Add the water to the yeast and stir until the yeast has dissolved. Add the egg to the yeast solution and mix. This is the wet mixture. Add the dry mixture to the wet mixture. Mix with a wooden spoon and then your hands to form a dough.

Turn the dough out onto a floured surface. Knead for 10 minutes, until the dough is smooth and elastic. Place the dough back in the bowl, cover and leave for about 1 hour, or until doubled in volume.

Turn the dough out onto a floured surface, and punch it down gently, to release the air. Cut the dough into 9 equal portions and roll them into balls. Take each ball of dough and push your finger through the middle to make a neat hole. Place the bagels on the prepared baking sheet, cover and leave to rest for 10 minutes.

Half-fill a 2-litre/2-quart saucepan with water, add the remaining 1 teaspoon salt and bring to the boil. Cook the bagels, in batches of 3, until they rise up. Turn the bagels over and boil for 5 minutes more. Transfer the bagels to the baking sheet to cool slightly.

Preheat the oven to 240°C (475°F) Gas 9. Place a roasting pan at the bottom of the oven. Fill a cup with water and set aside. Brush egg wash over the bagels, and dip in poppy or sesame seeds, if you like. Place the bagels in the oven, pour the cupful of water onto the hot roasting pan and lower the temperature to 200°C (400°F) Gas 6. Bake for 15 minutes, or until golden brown. Tap the bottom of a bagel – if it sounds hollow, it is done. Set on a wire rack to cool.

300 ml/1¼ cups hand-hot water

15 g/3 teaspoons fresh yeast*

500 g/4 cups ciabatta flour or white strong/bread flour

2 teaspoons fine sea salt

60 ml/4 tablespoons extra virgin olive oil

Biga (aged-dough starter)

250 g/2 cups white strong/bread flour

5 g/1 teaspoon fresh yeast*

150 ml/⅔ cup hand-hot water

2 baking sheets, heavily floured

Makes 12 rolls

* If using instant easy-blend/rapid-rise dried yeast, mix one-third of a 7 g/¼ oz. packet with the flour to make the biga, then work in the water. Finish the biga as in the main recipe. To make the ciabatta dough, add the water to the biga and work in to make a batter. Then mix half the flour with one 7 g/¼ oz. packet of instant easy-blend/rapid-rise dried yeast, add to the batter, and finish as in the main recipe.

Ciabatta comes from Northern Italy. It has a floury crust, a moist open texture and a good flavour of fruity olive oil. For the best results, use Italian ciabatta flour, which creates the large air bubbles needed for the characteristic texture.

ciabatta rolls

To make the biga, put the flour in a large bowl and make a well in the centre. Crumble the yeast into the well, then pour in the water. Mix the yeast with the water, then work in the flour to make a firm dough. Turn out onto a floured work surface, knead for 2 minutes, then return to the bowl and cover. Leave at room temperature for 8–12 hours – it will rise enormously, then fall back.

To make the ciabatta dough, put the water in a bowl and crumble the yeast over the top. Stir well until dispersed. Add to the biga and work into the dough by stirring with your fingers to make a thick, smooth batter. Work in half the flour to make a very sticky dough, then mix with your hands for 5 minutes until the dough has been thoroughly stretched and is elastic. Cover and leave to rise in a warm place for 2 hours, or until about 2½ times its original size.

Add the salt and olive oil, then gradually work in the rest of the flour to make a soft, sticky dough. Knead until smooth and elastic, then cover and leave to rise for 1 hour, or until doubled in volume.

Preheat the oven to 230°C (450°F) Gas 8.

Turn out the dough onto a floured surface, divide into 12 pieces and transfer to the baking sheets, spacing well apart. Shape into rough-looking rolls. Dust with flour, then cover and leave to rise for 30 minutes, until almost doubled in size. Bake for 15–20 minutes, or until golden brown. Tap the bottom of a roll – if it sounds hollow, it is done. Set the rolls on a wire rack to cool. Best eaten while still slightly warm or within 1 day.

cornmeal buns

Cornmeal 'mush'

150 g/1 generous cup coarse ground cornmeal/polenta

30 g/2 tablespoons lard or butter

60 g/¼ cup honey or molasses

250 ml/1 cup milk

Dough

500 g/4 cups white or wholemeal/whole-wheat strong/bread flour

2.5 g/1¼ teaspoons instant easy-blend/rapid-rise yeast, 5 g/1¾ teaspoons dried/active dry yeast, or 10 g/2 teaspoons fresh yeast

2½ teaspoons salt

150 ml/⅔ cup water

Glaze

1 egg

1 teaspoon water

a pinch of salt

a pinch of sugar

Decoration

a little cornmeal/polenta

2 baking sheets, greased and lined with parchment paper

Makes 18 buns

Cornmeal makes an excellent addition to bread and buns. Using it with wheat flour creates a bread or bun that is light with great flavour. These are delicious at breakfast with honey.

For the cornmeal 'mush', put the cornmeal/polenta into a bowl and add the lard or butter and the honey or molasses. Heat the milk to just below boiling point, then pour it into the bowl. Stir it around to melt the fat and mix everything up. Leave to cool completely.

For the dough, put the flour into a big mixing bowl. If you are using instant easy-blend/rapid-rise or fresh yeast, simply sprinkle it into the bowl with the flour, add all of the remaining ingredients, including the cornmeal 'mush', and mix it together into a ball.

If you are using dried/active dry yeast, make a well in the flour and sprinkle in the yeast. Add the water and leave for 15 minutes. Add the other ingredients, including the cornmeal 'mush', and mix it together into a ball.

Turn the dough onto a floured surface, and knead for 10 minutes, until smooth. Place it back in the bowl, cover and leave for 2 hours.

Turn the dough out onto a floured surface, and punch it down gently, to release the air. Divide the dough into 18 portions. Shape each of these into a tight ball. Place on the prepared baking sheets, cover and allow them to rest for 1 hour.

Preheat the oven to 220°C (425°F) Gas 7.

Beat all the glaze ingredients together, and brush over the buns. Sprinkle cornmeal/polenta over them. Bake in the preheated oven for 20 minutes, or until golden brown. Tap the bottom of a bun – if it sounds hollow, it is done. Set the buns on a wire rack to cool.

oat baps

200 g/2 cups porridge/rolled oats, plus extra for dusting

300 g/2½ cups plain/all-purpose flour

1 teaspoon salt

1 teaspoon bicarbonate of soda/baking soda, sifted

400 ml/scant 1¾ cups whole/full-fat milk

2 teaspoons freshly squeezed lemon juice

baking sheet, greased

Makes 8 baps

The bap is one of the glories of British baking and in Scotland, the oat capital of the world, they are made with crunchy rolled oats.

Preheat the oven to 190°C (375°F) Gas 5.

Put the dry ingredients in a food processor and process to make a fairly coarse mixture. Mix the milk with the lemon juice, then with the machine running, slowly pour the liquid through the feed tube to make a soft but not sticky dough.

Turn the dough out onto a surface dusted with oats, then roll or pat the dough into a round loaf about 23 cm/9 in. in diameter and 5 cm/2 in. thick.

Put the dough on the prepared baking sheet and, using a sharp knife, score it into 8 wedges.

Bake in the preheated oven for about 20 minutes, until firm to the touch and lightly browned underneath. Cool slightly on a wire rack. Eat while still warm, or split and toast.

These individual baguettes are always a hit at summer picnics. They go well with soft cheese, such as Brie, and if you can get your hands on a jar of lingonberry jam, spoon some of that on top of the Brie.

rye baguettes

250 ml/1 cup plus 1 tablespoon hand-hot water

7-g/¼-oz. packet instant easy-blend/rapid-rise yeast

1 teaspoon salt

300 g/2½ cups white strong/ bread flour

100 g/¾ cup wholemeal/ whole-wheat rye flour

1 tablespoon rapeseed oil (or vegetable oil)

2 tablespoons golden/light corn syrup

50 g/⅓ cup (dark) raisins, chopped

2 baking sheets, greased and lined with parchment paper

Makes 8 small baguettes

Put the water in a large mixing bowl with the yeast and whisk until it has dissolved. Add the salt and flours, and mix quickly into a soft dough.

Turn the dough out onto a lightly floured surface and knead for 2–3 minutes. Return to the bowl and add the remaining ingredients, then knead for 2–3 minutes again. You should now have a firm dough. Sprinkle with flour, cover and leave to prove for 1 hour, or until the dough has doubled in volume.

Turn the dough out onto a floured surface, and punch it down gently, to release the air. Divide it into eight portions. Roll each portion into a baguette, about 4 cm/1¾ in. wide in the middle and slightly pointed at the ends. Arrange on the prepared baking trays. Cover and leave to prove for 1 hour, or until the baguettes have doubled in size.

Preheat the oven to 240°C (475°F) Gas 9.

Dip a sharp knife in cold water and use to make 3 diagonal cuts on top of each baguette. Bake in the preheated oven for 10–12 minutes, or until golden brown. Tap the bottom of a baguette – if it sounds hollow, it is done. Set the baguettes on a wire rack to cool.

little spring onion breads

These tiny rounds of dough, flavoured with chopped spring onions, are made and baked in minutes. Serve as a nibble with drinks or as an appetizer, with olives, salami, prosciutto, soft cheese and your favourite selection of antipasti.

125 g/1 cup minus 1 tablespoon self-raising/self-rising flour

¼ teaspoon salt

2 spring onions/scallions, finely chopped

2 tablespoons olive oil

1 large/US extra large egg

2 teaspoons sesame seeds

freshly ground black pepper

5-cm/2-in round cookie cutter (optional)

baking sheet, greased

Makes 12 very small rolls

Preheat the oven to 190°C (375°F) Gas 5.

In a large bowl, mix the flour with the salt, 3 grinds of pepper and the spring onions/scallions. In a separate bowl, whisk the olive oil with the egg and 1 tablespoon water, then add to the dry ingredients. Work the mixture with your hands to make a soft dough. If there are dry crumbs in the bowl, add more water, a teaspoonful at a time.

Turn the dough out onto a floured surface, and knead for 10 seconds to make a smooth ball. Cover with a damp tea towel/kitchen towel and leave for 2–3 minutes. Knead for a couple more seconds, then roll out to about 5 mm/¼ in. thickness.

Stamp out rounds with a cookie cutter or an upturned glass, and set them slightly apart on the prepared baking sheet. Gather up the trimmings and re-roll them to make more rounds. Sprinkle with the sesame seeds.

Bake in the preheated oven for 8–10 minutes, or until golden brown and firm to the touch.

Serve warm from the oven. Best eaten the same day but can be frozen for up to 1 month. Thaw and gently reheat before serving.

Variation

Omit the spring onions/scallions and use either 1 rounded tablespoon chopped sun-dried tomatoes or 1 tablespoon snipped chives or freshly chopped flat leaf parsley.

Crispy on the outside and soft on the inside, the loaves in this chapter are ideal for serving alongside soups and salads. Tear them into chunks while still slightly warm from the oven, and smear with butter or dip them in olive oil.

rustic loaves

baguettes

This is the traditional way of making baguettes, using the 'poolish' (pre-ferment) method whereby a wet sponge is left to ferment overnight before the rest of the ingredients are added. It is worth the time and effort for the flavour it produces.

300 g/2⅓ cups plain/all-purpose flour or French T55 flour

1 teaspoon salt

2 g/½ teaspoon fresh yeast or 1 g/¼ teaspoon dried/active dry yeast

140 ml/½ cup plus 1 tablespoon warm water

Poolish

2 g/½ teaspoon fresh yeast or 1 g/¼ teaspoon dried/active dry yeast

125 ml/½ cup warm water

125 g/1 cup plain/all-purpose flour or French T55 flour

proofing linen or tea towel/ kitchen towel

floured long baguette bread peel (optional)

baking sheet, lined with parchment paper

Makes 3 baguettes

Start by making the poolish. In a mixing bowl, weigh out the yeast, add the water and stir until the yeast has dissolved. Add the flour and mix with a wooden spoon until a smooth paste forms. Cover the bowl and let ferment overnight at room temperature.

The next day, in a mixing bowl, mix the flour and the salt together and set aside. This is the dry mixture.

In another mixing bowl, weigh out the yeast, add the water and stir until the yeast has dissolved. Mix the yeast solution into the poolish, then add the dry mixture. Mix with a wooden spoon and then your hands to form a dough.

Turn the dough out onto a floured surface. Knead for 10 minutes, until the dough is smooth and elastic. Place the dough back in the bowl, cover and leave for about 1 hour, or until doubled in volume.

Turn the dough out onto a floured surface, and punch it down gently, to release the air. Divide into 3 portions – weigh each piece to check they are even.

Gently flatten each ball of dough into an oval. Pull both ends of the oval out, then fold them over into the middle. You will now have a roughly rectangular shape. Pull and fold the top of the rectangle one third of the way towards the middle, pressing it into the dough. Swivel it 180° and repeat. Repeat until you have a neat, long loaf shape. Repeat with the remaining portions of dough. Cover the loaves (seam-side down) and leave to rest for 15 minutes.

Turn one loaf over and flatten slightly. Fold the top right of the rectangle one third of the way towards the middle, pressing it into the dough. Repeat with the top left and repeat until rolled up. Roll the dough between your hands until you get a baguette about the length of your baking sheet. Repeat with the remaining dough.

Dust the proofing linen or tea towel/kitchen towel with flour and lay it on the baking sheet. Arrange the baguettes on the cloth, seam-side up, pulling a bit of excess cloth between each baguette to separate them. Cover with the cloth and leave to rise for about 1 hour, or until doubled in size.

About 20 minutes before baking, preheat the oven to 240°C (475°F) Gas 9. Place a roasting pan at the bottom of the oven. Fill a cup with water and set aside.

When the dough has finished rising, turn the baguettes over with a peel, if using, onto the lined baking sheet. Dust them with flour and slash along their lengths using a serrated knife.

Put in the preheated oven and pour the reserved cupful of water onto the hot roasting pan. Bake for 10–15 minutes, or until golden brown. To check if baked through, tip one baguette upside down and tap the bottom – it should sound hollow. Set the baguettes on a wire rack to cool.

ciabatta

This popular Italian bread is named after its characteristic appearance, *ciabatta* being the Italian word for 'slipper'. Time and patience (and olive oil!) are needed to create those lovely bubbles in the loaf. It is best served warm, dipped in olive oil and balsamic vinegar or slathered with butter.

200 g/1⅔ cups white strong/bread flour or Italian '00' flour

¾ teaspoon salt

2 g/½ teaspoon fresh yeast or 1 g/¼ teaspoon dried/active dry yeast

150 ml/⅔ cup warm water

about 3 tablespoons olive oil

baking sheet, lined with parchment paper

Makes 2 small ciabattas

In one mixing bowl, mix the flour and salt together and set aside. This is the dry mixture. In another mixing bowl, weigh out the yeast. Add the water and stir until the yeast has dissolved. This is the wet mixture. Add the dry mixture to the wet mixture. Mix with a wooden spoon until you get a fairly sticky dough.

Put about one-third of the olive oil in another large mixing bowl and place the sticky dough in it. Cover and leave to rest for 1 hour. After 1 hour, gently fold the dough twice. Cover and leave to rest again, then repeat this process three times, adding a little olive oil before resting the dough each time so that it does not stick too much to the bottom of the bowl. At the end of the resting cycle, the dough should be well risen and bubbly.

Transfer the dough to a floured surface. Be gentle so that you do not damage the air bubbles. Divide the dough into 2 equal portions using a sharp, serrated knife. Mould each portion of dough into a slipper shape. Roll each ciabatta in flour, then place on the prepared baking sheet. Leave to rest for 5–10 minutes.

Meanwhile, preheat the oven to 240°C (475°F) Gas 9.

Bake the ciabattas in the preheated oven for about 15 minutes, or until golden brown. Tap the bottom of one loaf – if it sounds hollow, it is done. Set the ciabattas on a wire rack to cool. (Do not bake for too long – ciabatta should be very soft on the inside with only a thin crust.)

450 g/3¾ cups white strong/bread flour

2 teaspoons salt

7-g/¼-oz. packet instant easy-blend/fast-action yeast

1 teaspoon sugar

3 tablespoons olive oil

250 ml/1 cup plus 1 tablespoon lukewarm water

Topping

olive oil, for drizzling

several large pinches of sea salt flakes

100 g/⅔ cup cherry tomatoes

2 tablespoons pesto

a handful of fresh rosemary needles

1 red onion, thinly sliced

Makes 1 loaf

This soft focaccia-style bread is a great accompaniment to soup or salad. You can add your choice of flavoursome toppings, from simple sea salt flakes and fresh rosemary needles, to cherry tomatoes, red onion and fresh pesto.

tomato and pesto bread

Put the flour and salt in a large bowl and mix together. Stir the dried yeast and sugar through the flour and set aside. Make a well in the centre of the flour and add the olive oil. Then add 185 ml/ ¾ cup of the water. Quickly stir together to form a soft dough. If the dough seems dry, add the remaining water.

Turn the dough out onto a floured surface and knead for about 10 minutes until the dough becomes smooth and elastic. Place the dough back in the bowl, cover and leave for about 45 minutes, or until doubled in volume.

Turn the dough out onto a floured surface, and punch it down gently, to release the air. Sprinkle some flour on a baking sheet and stretch out your dough into a large rectangle, about 2 cm/ ¾ in. thick. Cover with oiled clingfilm/plastic wrap and set aside to rise for 30–40 minutes, or until the dough has doubled in size and, if you make an indent, it will spring back half way.

Preheat the oven to 200°C (400°F) Gas 6.

Use a finger to dimple the top of the dough all over – press your finger into the dough to make regular indents until the whole loaf is a mass of dimples, then sprinkle the bread with olive oil and salt flakes. Add the cherry tomatoes, pesto and rosemary. Bake in the top of the oven for 10 minutes, then add the sliced onion. Put it back in the oven for 15–20 minutes. It should be fairly well risen and golden brown, and feel quite light when you pick it up. Tap the bottom of the bread – if it sounds hollow, it is done. Set the bread on a wire rack to cool.

olive and herb bread

Olives give a great Mediterranean flavour to bread, and work especially well with mixed herbs. A mixture of olives gives the best taste, but you can use just one type, if you prefer.

40 g/¼ cup green pitted olives or green olives stuffed with pimento

40 g/¼ cup black pitted olives

1 teaspoon mixed dried herbs, e.g. herbes de Provence

250 g/2 cups white strong/bread flour

¾ teaspoon salt

3 g/⅔ teaspoon fresh yeast or 2 g/¾ teaspoon dried/active dry yeast

180 ml/¾ cup warm water

baking sheet, lined with parchment paper

Makes 1 small loaf

Mix the olives with the herbs and set aside.

In one mixing bowl, mix the flour and salt together and set aside. This is the dry mixture. In another mixing bowl, weigh out the yeast. Add the water and stir until the yeast has dissolved. This is the wet mixture. Add the dry mixture to the wet mixture. Mix with a wooden spoon and then your hands to form a dough.

Add the olive mixture to the dough. Turn the dough out onto a floured surface. Knead for 10 minutes, until the dough is smooth and elastic. Place the dough back in the bowl, cover and leave for about 1 hour, or until doubled in volume.

Turn the dough out onto a floured surface, and punch it down gently, to release the air. Gently pull it into a long rectangle. Fold the left-hand third of the rectangle over towards the right. Now fold the right-hand third over. Press down slightly to seal the dough together. You will now have a neat rectangular loaf shape. Turn the loaf over and place on the prepared baking sheet. Dust with flour. Cover the loaf and leave to rise for 30–45 minutes, or until almost doubled in size.

Preheat the oven to 240°C (475°F) Gas 9. Place a roasting pan at the bottom of the oven. Fill a cup with water and set aside.

Place the loaf in the preheated oven, pour the reserved cupful of water into the hot roasting pan and lower the oven temperature to 200°C (400°F) Gas 6. Bake the bread for about 35 minutes, or until golden brown. Tap the bottom of the loaf – if it sounds hollow, it is done. Set the loaf on a wire rack to cool.

Adding grated courgettes and ricotta to this loaf makes it light and moist with a chewy texture. You can vary the herbs according to taste, but parsley, chervil and a little tarragon or dill is a good place to start.

courgette and ricotta loaf

200 g/7 oz. courgettes/zucchini, topped, tailed and coarsely grated

1¼ teaspoons salt

400 g/3⅓ cups white strong/bread flour, plus extra if needed

100 g/¾ cup spelt flour

3 g/1½ teaspoons instant easy-blend/rapid-rise dried yeast

2–3 tablespoons chopped herbs of your choice

½ teaspoon sugar

200 ml/1 cup minus 2 tablespoons hand-hot water

120 g/generous ½ cup ricotta or sieved/strained cottage cheese, well-drained

80 g/1 generous cup freshly grated Parmesan cheese

1 tablespoon olive oil

sea salt

baking sheet, floured

Makes 1 large loaf

Put the grated courgettes/zucchini in a bowl and toss with 1 teaspoon of the salt. Put in a colander to drain for 30–40 minutes, then squeeze out the excess water with your hands. Put the flours in a large bowl, and add the yeast and the rest of the salt. Stir in the herbs and grated courgettes/zucchini.

Dissolve the sugar in the water, then add to the flour mixture with the cheese, Parmesan and the oil. Start to bring together to form a dough. You might need a little extra flour if the dough is too sticky, but do not add too much. Cover and allow to rest for 10 minutes.

Turn the dough out onto a floured surface. Knead for 5 minutes, until smooth and elastic. (As you knead, the dough will get stickier as the courgettes give up their moisture, so add a dusting of flour, but again, not too much.) Put the dough into a lightly oiled bowl, cover and leave to rise for about 90 minutes, until doubled in size. Then knock it back to deflate, knead gently for a few seconds, then cover again and let it rise for about 40 minutes.

Turn the dough out onto a floured surface, and punch it down gently, to release the air. Shape into a round and score the top in a criss-cross pattern with a sharp knife. Put on the prepared baking sheet, cover and let it rise for 30–40 minutes.

Preheat the oven to 220°C (425°F) Gas 7. Dust the top of the loaf with some extra flour, then bake in the preheated oven for about 40 minutes, until golden brown. Tap the bottom of the loaf – if it sounds hollow, it is done. Set the loaf on a wire rack to cool.

Mediterranean bread

The bitterness of olives combines with the creamy feta and sweet sun-blushed tomatoes in this delicious loaf. Start this bread the night before you plan to bake it.

400 ml/scant 1¾ cups hand-hot water

2 7-g/¼-oz. packets instant easy-blend/rapid-rise yeast

625 g/5 cups white strong/bread flour

50 g/⅓ cup dried milk powder/non-fat dry milk

1½ tablespoons sugar

1 egg, beaten

2 good pinches of sea salt

180 g/1 cup pitted black olives, roughly chopped

a handful of fresh rosemary or basil, roughly chopped

1 large dried red chilli, chopped

200 g/7 oz. drained sun-blushed/half-dried tomatoes, roughly chopped

1 tablespoon olive oil

200 g/7 oz. feta cheese, crumbled

large baking sheet, greased and lined with parchment paper

Makes 2 loaves

Combine the water and the yeast in a large mixing bowl then sift in the flour followed by the milk powder, sugar, beaten egg and lastly the salt. Using a spatula, mix the ingredients together well.

Add the chopped olives, herbs, chilli and sun-blushed/half-dried tomatoes, mixing well. Place a clean tea towel/kitchen towel over the bowl and allow the dough to rest for about 15 minutes.

Turn the dough out onto a floured surface and knead gently for 10 minutes. Drizzle the olive oil into the mixing bowl, greasing it all over, then return the dough to the bowl, cover and leave to rise for 8 hours or overnight.

Turn the dough out onto a floured surface, and punch it down gently, to release the air. Knead a few times, then cut the dough into 2 equal portions and return one of them to the mixing bowl. Sprinkle half of the crumbled feta cheese onto the dough in front of you and really work it into the dough. Flatten the dough out into a rectangle and cut it in half lengthways. With the palm of your hand, roll each half into a long sausage, about 55 cm/22 in. long and 5 cm/2 in. thick, then twist the 2 sausages together while also coiling the dough around into a tight circle. Repeat this process with the other half of dough in the bowl.

Lay the loaves onto the baking sheet, cover with parchment paper, then a tea towel/kitchen towel. Leave to rise for 1 hour.

Preheat the oven to 180°C (350°F) Gas 4.

Bake the loaves for 25–30 minutes, until golden brown. Tap the bottom of a loaf – if it sounds hollow, it is done. Cool on a wire rack.

This is a simple yet delicious rustic loaf flavoured with fresh sage. It is particularly good served warm from the oven and is the perfect accompaniment to hearty winter soups and stews. It works well with pumpkin or butternut squash dishes as the musky sage complements their sweetness perfectly.

Tuscan fresh sage and olive oil bread

375 g/3 cups plus 2 tablespoons plain/all-purpose flour

125 g/1 cup minus 1 tablespoon wholemeal/whole-wheat flour

2 teaspoons freshly chopped sage leaves

1 tablespoon baking powder

½ teaspoon salt

2 large/US extra large eggs

3 tablespoons olive oil

about 175 ml/¾ cup milk

baking sheet, lightly greased

Makes 1 medium loaf

Preheat the oven to 180°C (350°F) Gas 4.

Mix the flours with the chopped sage leaves, baking powder and salt in a large bowl. This is the dry mixture. In a separate bowl, lightly beat the eggs with the olive oil and milk. This is the wet mixture. Add the dry mixture to the wet mixture. Mix with a wooden spoon and then your hands to form a soft and slightly sticky dough. If there are dry crumbs or the dough feels stiff, work in a little more milk.

Turn out the dough onto a lightly floured surface and shape into a ball about 18 cm/7 in. across. Put it on the prepared baking sheet and score the top with a sharp knife.

Put in the oven immediately and bake for about 45 minutes, or until golden brown. Tap the bottom of the loaf – if it sounds hollow, it is done. Set the loaf on a wire rack to cool. Break into quarters or cut into slices. This loaf is best eaten the same day.

Variation

To make an **Olive and Rosemary Bread**, follow the same method as above, replacing the chopped sage with 1 teaspoon freshly chopped rosemary needles, and adding about 75 g/½ cup roughly chopped pitted black and green olives.

Focaccia is made with the same dough as ciabatta, but can then be used as a base for some delicious toppings. Tear into chunks and enjoy at a picnic or on a long car trip.

focaccia

200 g/1⅔ cups white strong/ bread flour or Italian '00' flour

¾ teaspoon salt

2 g/½ teaspoon fresh yeast or 1 g/¼ teaspoon dried/active dry yeast

150 ml/⅔ cup warm water

about 3 tablespoons olive oil, plus extra to drizzle

toppings of your choice, e.g. fresh rosemary sprigs and coarse sea salt; or thinly sliced red onion and pieces of cooked potato; or pitted Kalamata olives; or halved cherry tomatoes and half-dried tomatoes

baking sheet, lined with parchment paper

Makes 1 focaccia

In one mixing bowl, mix the flour and salt together. This is the dry mixture. In another mixing bowl, weigh out the yeast. Add the water and stir until the yeast has dissolved. This is the wet mixture. Add the dry mixture to the wet mixture. Mix with a wooden spoon and then your hands to form a dough.

Put a tablespoon of the olive oil in another large mixing bowl and place the sticky dough in it. Cover and leave to rest for 1 hour. After 1 hour, gently fold the dough twice. Cover again.

Repeat this process three times, adding a little olive oil before resting the dough each time so that it does not stick too much to the bowl. At the very end of the resting cycle, the dough should be well risen and bubbly. Transfer the dough to the prepared baking sheet. Be gentle so that you do not damage the air bubbles. Cover and leave to rest for 10 minutes.

Push the dough out with your fingertips to flatten it and widen it into a rough square. Cover and leave to rest for 10 minutes.

Arrange the toppings on the focaccia, pressing them into the dough slightly. (If you are using olives, arrange them over one half of the focaccia, then fold over and press lightly. This will prevent the olives from burning in the oven.) Drizzle over a little olive oil. Cover and leave to rise for 20 minutes, or until doubled in volume.

Preheat the oven to 240°C (475°F) Gas 9.

Bake the focaccia in the preheated oven for 15–20 minutes, or until golden brown. Tap the bottom of the loaf – if it sounds hollow, it is done. Set the focaccia on a wire rack to cool.

pizza dough

This recipe makes five individual bases – just add your favourite toppings. Start the day before you want to bake them.

500 g/4 cups white strong/bread flour

2 teaspoons salt

2 g/½ teaspoon fresh yeast or 1 g/¼ teaspoon dried/active dry yeast

250 ml/1 cup warm water

toppings of your choice, e.g. mozzarella, fresh sage, drizzle of olive oil and sea salt

baking stone (optional)

Makes 5 pizza bases

In one mixing bowl, mix the flour and salt together. This is the dry mixture. In another mixing bowl, weigh out the yeast. Add the water to the yeast, and stir until the yeast has dissolved. This is the wet mixture. Add the dry mixture to the wet mixture. Mix with a wooden spoon and then your hands to form a dough.

Turn the dough out onto a floured surface. Knead for 10 minutes, until the dough is smooth and elastic. Place the dough back in the bowl, cover and leave for 24 hours, or until doubled in volume.

The next day when the dough has doubled in volume, turn it out onto a floured surface, and punch it down gently, to release the air. Divide the dough into 5 equal portions. Take one portion of dough and roll between your hands until you get a round, smooth ball. Flatten one side slightly and lay it, flat-side down, on the work surface. Repeat with the remaining portions of dough. Cover the balls of dough with a large bowl. Leave to rest for 10 minutes.

Roll out each ball of dough with a rolling pin until as thin as you like. Prick all over with a fork. Lay each base on a sheet of parchment paper and arrange the toppings of your choice over the top, then leave to rest for 10–15 minutes.

Preheat the oven to 240°C (475°F) Gas 9. Set a baking sheet or baking stone in the oven to preheat. Place a roasting pan at the bottom of the oven. Fill a cup with water and set aside.

Add any toppings to your pizza, then place on the preheated baking sheet or stone, keeping the pizza on the parchment paper. Pour the cupful of water into the hot roasting pan to form steam and lower the oven temperature to 220°C (425°F) Gas 7. Bake for about 15 minutes, or until the edges are golden.

This is an unyeasted bread from Umbria, and very quick to make. When making this type of bread, work quickly, because as soon as the liquid comes into contact with the baking powder, a chemical reaction starts to aerate the bread. Use a light hand and get the dough into the oven as soon as possible.

300 g/2½ cups Italian '00' flour or plain/all-purpose flour

1 teaspoon baking powder

1 teaspoon salt

50 g/¾ cup freshly grated Parmesan cheese, plus extra for sprinkling

50 g/3½ tablespoons butter, melted and cooled

100–150 ml/7–10 tablespoons milk

2 eggs

baking stone (optional)

baking sheet, lined with parchment paper

Makes 1 medium loaf

parmesan soda bread

Put the baking stone or a large, heavy baking sheet on the lower shelf of the oven. Preheat the oven to 190°C (375°F) Gas 5.

Sift the flour, baking powder and salt into a medium mixing bowl. Stir in the Parmesan and make a well in the centre.

Whisk the cooled, melted butter with 100 ml/7 tablespoons of the milk and the eggs, and pour into the well. Mix until just combined – overmixing will make the bread tough. The dough should be quite soft; if it isn't, add a little more milk. Turn out onto a floured work surface and knead briefly. Put the ball of dough directly onto the lined baking sheet. Pat into a disc about 3 cm/1¼ in. thick. Brush with a little extra milk, then mark into wedges with the back of a knife and sprinkle with Parmesan.

Working quickly, open the oven door and slide paper and bread onto the hot baking stone or baking sheet. If you are brave, try to shoot the bread into the oven so that it leaves the paper behind – this takes practice!

Bake for 15 minutes, then very carefully slide the bread out and remove the baking paper. Bake for a further 5 minutes or until the crust is golden. Remove from the oven and wrap in a clean tea towel/kitchen towel. Serve warm, broken into wedges, ready to split and fill.

From puffy pitas to crisp grissini, the recipes in this chapter are perfect accompaniments to all sorts of meals. Whether you want something for dipping or scooping or topping with cheese, the ideal recipe is here.

flatbreads and breadsticks

barley flatbreads

These flatbreads are really quick and easy to make – this is 'fast food' at its best! Eat them any way you like, or try them straight out of the oven when a pat of butter melts invitingly on top. You can also eat them with honey, or top them with Jarlsberg cheese or honey-roast ham.

225 g/2 cups minus 2 tablespoons barley flour

1 teaspoon salt

200 ml/1 cup minus 2 tablespoons very cold water

baking sheet, lined with parchment paper

Makes 4 flatbreads

Preheat the oven to 240°C (475°F) Gas 9.

Mix the flour and salt together in a mixing bowl. Add the cold water and mix quickly into a firm dough.

Divide the dough into four, and roll into balls between your hands. Place on the prepared baking sheet and flatten with your hands or a floured rolling pin until about 12 cm/5 in. in diameter and 5 mm/¼ in. thick.

Bake the flatbreads in the preheated oven for 15 minutes, or until golden brown.

rye pockets

When baked, these little breads puff up and become hollow, making them perfect for filling.

1 tablespoon honey

100 ml/⅓ cup plus 1 tablespoon boiling water

150 ml/⅔ cup milk

50 g/10 teaspoons fresh yeast

1 teaspoon sea salt

25 g/¼ cup rye flakes

150 g/1¼ cups wholemeal/ whole-wheat rye flour

50 g/generous ⅓ cup barley flour

200 g/1¼ cups white strong/ bread flour

1 teaspoon ground cumin

3½ tablespoons sunflower/ safflower oil

Makes 18 pockets

Put the honey and water in a large bowl and stir. Add the milk. Crumble the yeast into the warm liquid, then add the salt, rye flakes, rye flour and barley flour, and whisk to combine. Add the strong/bread flour and cumin, and mix with a wooden spoon. Add the oil and knead in until smooth.

Cover and leave to rise for 30–60 minutes, or until doubled in volume.

Preheat the oven to 240°C (475°F) Gas 9 and put a baking sheet in to heat up.

Pull off pieces of dough the size of plums and roll into balls. You should make 18 balls. Place the balls on sheets of parchment paper that will fit on your baking sheet, and flatten with your hands or a rolling pin to make discs about 5 mm/¼ in. thick. Cover and leave for 10–15 minutes, until slightly risen.

Slide one sheet of parchment paper onto the hot tray (you will need to bake in batches) and bake at the top of the oven for 10 minutes, or until risen and golden brown. These are best eaten when freshly baked.

Pita breads are quite exciting to watch in the oven – they puff up in no time – and make perfect pockets for stuffing with all sorts of delicious fillings.

pita breads

200 g/1⅔ cups plain/all-purpose flour

¾ teaspoon salt

2 g/½ teaspoon fresh or 1 g/¼ teaspoon dried/active dry yeast

120 ml/½ cup warm water

Makes 6 mini pita breads

In one mixing bowl, mix the flour and salt together and set aside. This is the dry mixture. In another mixing bowl, weigh out the yeast. Add the water and stir until the yeast has dissolved. This is the wet mixture. Add the dry mixture to the wet mixture. Mix with a wooden spoon and then your hands to form a dough.

Turn the dough out onto a floured surface. Knead for 10 minutes, until the dough is smooth and elastic. Place the dough back in the bowl, cover and leave for about 1 hour, or until doubled in volume.

Turn the dough out onto a floured surface, and punch it down gently, to release the air. Divide the dough into 6 equal portions using a sharp, serrated knife. Take one portion of dough and roll between your hands to make a ball. Repeat with the remaining dough. Cover and leave to rest for 10 minutes.

Preheat the oven to 240°C (475°F) Gas 9 and place a baking sheet on the middle rack to preheat.

Using a rolling pin, roll out each ball. Cover and leave to rise for 10 minutes.

Dust the pita breads with flour and place on the preheated baking sheet in the oven. Bake until puffed up. The time will vary, so keep an eye on them. Don't worry if they are no longer round when baked – the important thing is that they puff up! Set the pita breads to cool slightly on a wire rack, then place them, warm, in a food bag so that they don't dry out.

These naan are puffy and delicious, and are excellent served with curries. The dough is simply mixed, left to rest, then shaped quickly and, when supper is ready, cooked under a very hot grill and eaten straight away.

cracked pepper naan

In a large bowl, mix the flour, pepper and salt. Make a well in the centre and add the yogurt. Add the water to the bowl, a little at a time, working the ingredients together with your fingers to make a soft and slightly sticky dough. Work the dough in the bowl for a couple of seconds to make a ball.

Cover the bowl with a damp tea towel/kitchen towel and leave for 1 hour.

Heat the grill/broiler (and grill/broiler rack) to its highest setting. Gently melt the butter with the garlic in a small saucepan or in the microwave.

Turn out the dough onto a lightly floured surface and divide into 8 equal portions. With floured fingers, shape each piece into a ball, then gently flatten and press each portion into an oval about 10 x 7 cm/4 x 3 in. long.

Cook the naan, in batches, directly on the grill/broiler rack under the heated grill/broiler for about 2 minutes, or until the breads puff up and are lightly golden. Flip them over using kitchen tongs and cook the second side until flecked with brown spots (this will take about 1 minute). Remove from the grill and brush the top with the hot melted butter and garlic. Wrap in a warm, clean cloth and serve immediately.

250 g/2 cups plus 1 tablespoon self-raising/self-rising flour

½ teaspoon coarsely ground black pepper or cracked black peppercorns

½ teaspoon salt

2 generous tablespoons natural/plain yogurt (not fat-free)

about 115 ml/½ cup hand-hot water

50 g/3½ tablespoons unsalted butter

2 garlic cloves, crushed

Makes 8 naan

roti or chapati

Simple to prepare and speedy to make, this dough is best made several hours before the rotis are cooked in order to develop their flavour. The dough will keep in the fridge perfectly well for one or two days.

300 g/2½ cups wholemeal/whole-wheat flour

200 ml/1 cup minus 1 tablespoon water

1½ teaspoons salt

Makes 20 roti

Put all the ingredients in a bowl and mix them together. Turn out onto a floured surface and knead for 10 minutes, until smooth.

Place the dough back in the bowl, cover and leave to rest for at least 2 hours, but more if you have time.

Turn the dough out onto a floured surface. Divide the dough into 20 equal portions and roll them into balls. Cover with a tea towel/kitchen towel and allow to rest for 10–15 minutes.

On a floured surface, flatten each ball into a disc and then roll as thinly as possible with a rolling pin.

Heat a frying pan/skillet until hot. Place a roti in the pan and dry-fry for 10–15 seconds. Flip it over and cook for 10–15 seconds more, then repeat, frying it for 10–15 seconds on each side every time. The roti may or may not puff up in the pan. Remove from the pan and keep warm wrapped in a tea towel/kitchen towel while you make the rest of the rotis.

If you want a really puffy roti, you can buy a long-handled, wire contraption from any Indian store. Transfer a cooked roti to the base of the contraption and then place over the flame of your stove. The roti will puff up just like a football! Be careful when you open it up that you do not burn yourself with the steam.

To eat, tear the rotis into pieces and pick your food up in the pieces of bread. Indian food will never taste as nice again!

This recipe is based on a classic Indian gram flour bread. These flatbreads are ideal to serve with dips in place of pita breads. You can add a variety of spices or herbs to the dough – finely chopped rosemary and thyme or Indian spices if you are serving as an accompaniment to curries and dhals.

gluten-free flatbreads

200 g/1⅔ cups gluten-free plain/all-purpose flour

100 g/1¾ cups gram (chickpea) flour

1 teaspoon fine salt

1 tablespoon sunflower/safflower or vegetable oil, plus extra for cooking (optional)

1 generous tablespoon natural/plain yogurt

Makes 8 flatbreads

Sift the plain/all-purpose flour into a mixing bowl and add the gram flour and salt. Pour in the oil and yogurt, then add about 60–80 ml/¼–⅓ cup water gradually, mixing with your hands until you have a ball of dough – you may not need all of the water. The dough should not be sticky at all and should be firmer than normal bread dough.

Divide the dough into 8 balls of equal size (about the size of a golf ball). Put them on a floured surface and use a rolling pin to roll each ball out to a thin 20-cm/8-in. round.

Heat a dry frying pan/skillet until hot. Cook the breads one at a time for 2–3 minutes on one side then turn over and cook for a further 1–2 minutes on the other side, until lightly golden brown. If you wish, add a little oil to the pan towards the end of cooking so that the breads are lightly fried, which adds to the taste. For best cooking results, press down on the breads during cooking with a clean heatproof towel, which squeezes out the air and causes the breads to puff up slightly.

These breads are best eaten on the day they are made.

Variation

To make spiced flatbreads add ½ teaspoon ground chilli, 1 teaspoon ground cumin and 1 teaspoon ground coriander, or 1 teaspoon garam masala or medium curry powder to the dough. Check that your spices do not contain any gluten.

soft-shell tacos

Home-made tortillas taste wonderful, and they are surprisingly simple to make at home. Fill with spicy bean and vegetable salsa, and some fresh guacamole, for a delicious Mexican lunch.

260 g/2 cups plus 2 tablespoons fine cornmeal/polenta

130 g/1 cup spelt flour or unbleached plain/all-purpose flour, plus extra for kneading

1 teaspoon sea salt

3 g/1 teaspoon dried/active dry yeast

3 tablespoons sunflower/safflower oil

235 ml/1 cup lukewarm water

Makes 8–10 tacos

Mix all the dry ingredients well in a large bowl, then incorporate the oil. Add enough of the water to get a soft ball of dough.

Turn the dough out onto a floured surface, and knead it for a couple of minutes, adding flour when needed but keeping the dough soft.

Divide the dough in half, and form 2 cylinders with your hands. Cover with a tea towel/kitchen towel and leave to rest for 15 minutes.

Cut each cylinder into 4–5 equal pieces. With a rolling pin, roll out each tortilla to the size of a small dessert plate. Sprinkle with flour to avoid sticking. Remember not to place rolled tortillas on top of each other!

Heat a frying pan/skillet until hot. Place a tortilla in the hot frying pan/skillet and allow to cook for about 30 seconds, or until it begins to puff up with air pockets. Turn it over and cook for another 30 seconds. Repeat with the remaining tortillas. Keep the cooked tortillas covered with a tea towel/kitchen towel so that they stay warm and don't dry out.

These delicate, crisp flatbreads are perfect with a glass of wine as a snack or apéritif.

Armenian flatbreads

Start by making the infused oil. Mix the oil, water and garlic together in a small bowl and set aside to infuse.

In one mixing bowl, mix the flour and salt together, and set aside. This is the dry mixture. In another mixing bowl, mix the olive oil and water. This is the wet mixture. Add the dry mixture to the wet mixture. Mix with a wooden spoon to bring it together, then leave to stand for 5 minutes.

Turn the dough out onto a floured surface. Knead for 10 minutes, until the dough is smooth and elastic. Place the dough back in the bowl, cover and leave to rise for 30 minutes.

Divide the dough into 4 equal portions using a sharp, serrated knife. Lay out your 4 prepared baking sheets.

Put one portion of dough in the middle of one baking sheet. Press on it with your hand to flatten slightly, then start to pull the corners of the dough outwards. Keep pulling and stretching from each corner until you get a very thin, rough rectangle about the size of the baking sheet. Leave to rest for 15 minutes.

Preheat the oven to 180°C (350°F) Gas 4.

Meanwhile, repeat with the other portions of dough on the other baking sheets. If you find that the dough is breaking, stop and let it rest for a few minutes while you work on another portion of dough. When the dough has rested, brush the infused oil all over. Cut each flatbread into 6 using a sharp knife. Sprinkle the sliced onion and the seeds evenly over all the flatbreads. Bake the flatbreads in the preheated oven, in batches, for 5–10 minutes, or until golden brown. Set on wire racks to cool.

160 g/1⅓ cups white strong/bread flour

1 teaspoon salt

3 tablespoons olive oil

75 ml/⅓ cup water

½ onion, thinly sliced

Infused oil

2 tablespoons olive oil

2 tablespoons water

1 garlic clove, crushed

Sprinkling

poppy seeds

nigella seeds (black onion seeds)

sesame seeds

4 baking sheets, lined with parchment paper

Makes about 24 flatbreads

rye crispbreads

These thin crispbreads are very easy to prepare and ready in minutes. They are wonderfully versatile, so you can either serve them simply with cheese or butter, or as an accompaniment to soups. You can also make them in sticks and serve them as party food with dips. They taste great straight out of the oven, but you can let them dry out and store them in an airtight container for several weeks.

250 g/2 cups white strong/bread flour

200 g/1⅔ cups wholemeal/whole-wheat rye flour

1 teaspoon salt

100 g/1 stick minus 1 tablespoon unsalted butter, chilled and cubed

200 ml/1 cup minus 1 tablespoon milk

2 baking sheets, lined with parchment paper

Makes about 64 small crispbreads

Preheat the oven to 230°C (450°F) Gas 8.

Put the flours and salt in a mixing bowl and mix well. Add the cubed butter and rub in using your fingertips, until the mixture looks like fine breadcrumbs.

Gradually add the milk to the flour mixture, stirring with a round-bladed knife until a dough forms.

Turn the dough out onto a lightly floured surface and divide into four even portions. Roll out one portion of the dough very thinly with a rolling pin. (Cover the other portions with clingfilm/plastic wrap to prevent them from drying out).

Cut into about 16 rough shapes (about 10 x 5 cm/4 x 2 in.) and place on the prepared baking sheets. Prick a few holes in the dough with a fork.

Bake in the preheated oven for 4–5 minutes, or until starting to brown in parts. Be careful as the crispbreads burn very easily.

Repeat with the rest of the dough.

Swedish cracker bread

250 g/2 cups strong white/bread flour

500 g/4 cups light rye flour (if you cannot get light rye flour, sift some dark rye flour and save the bran and germ in the sieve/strainer for putting on your cereal, and use the light rye flour in the bowl for the crackers)

3.5 g/1¾ teaspoons instant easy-blend/rapid-rise yeast, 7 g/2¼ teaspoons dried/active dry yeast, or 15 g/3 teaspoons fresh yeast

500 ml/2 cups full-fat/whole milk

2 teaspoons salt

3 tablespoons clear honey

1 tablespoon ground anise (or cinnamon or cumin or coriander or ginger)

coarse sea salt, caraway seeds, black and white sesame seeds, poppy seeds and/or dried herbs (don't use cheese, as it will burn), to decorate

Swedish 'kruskavel' (textured rolling pin) (optional)

2 baking sheets, greased and lined with parchment paper

Makes 25–30 crackers

These crackers are crisp and tasty, and are the perfect partners for cheese. They are great for picnics and dipping.

If you are using instant easy-blend/rapid-rise or fresh yeast, put all the ingredients in a big bowl. Mix with a wooden spoon and then your hands to form a dough.

If you are using dried/active dry yeast, put the flour in a big bowl and make a well in the middle. Sprinkle the yeast in the well and add one-quarter of the milk. Cover and allow to rest for 15 minutes. Add the rest of the ingredients. Mix with a wooden spoon and then your hands to form a dough.

Put the dough back in the bowl, cover and allow to rest overnight.

The next day, turn the dough out onto a floured surface. Divide into 25–30 portions, about the size of golf balls. Cover with a tea towel/kitchen towel and allow to rest for 5 minutes.

Preheat the oven to 200°C (400°F) Gas 6.

On the floured surface, roll each portion of dough out extremely thinly. Traditionally you roll them into a round and use a cutter to cut a hole out of the middle so you can store them by threading a string through them and hanging them up, but you can cut any shapes you like. Prick the shapes with a fork, roll with a 'kruskavel' or thump gently with a meat tenderizer to create indentations.

Sprinkle the shapes with water and decorate with a bit of coarse sea salt and your choice of toppings. Place the shapes on the prepared baking sheets, about 1 cm/½ in. apart. Bake in the preheated oven for 10–12 minutes. Watch them carefully, as they burn in an instant! Allow to cool completely on a wire rack.

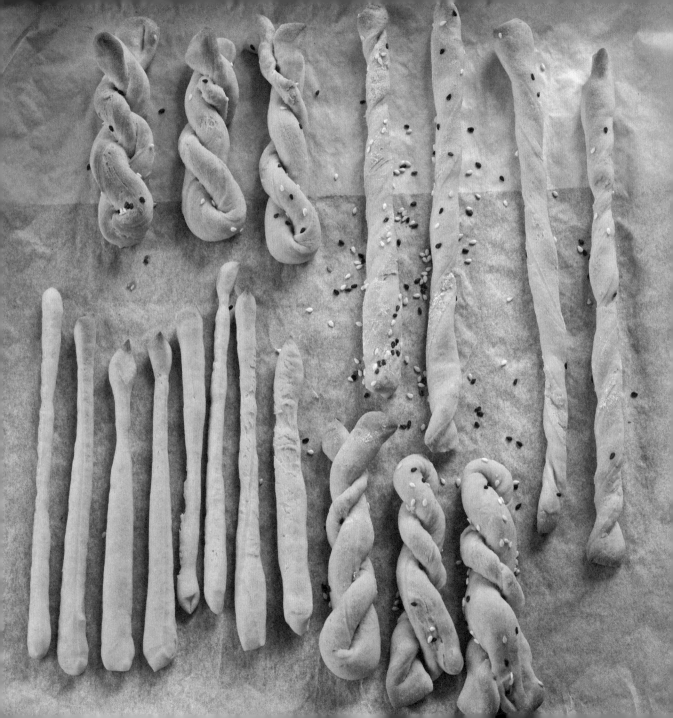

Should a breadstick be long, thin and crispy or short, fat and chewy? The answer is: you can have them any way you want. You can make them plain or you can twist them. You can roll them in polenta, sesame seeds or poppy seeds. You can do what you like – they are your grissini!

grissini

300 g/2½ cups plain/all-purpose white wheat flour

1.5 g/¾ teaspoon instant easy-blend/rapid-rise yeast, 3 g/1 teaspoon dried/active dry yeast, or 6 g/1⅓ teaspoons fresh yeast

200 ml/¾ cup plus 1 tablespoon water

1½ teaspoons salt

1 teaspoon malt syrup (optional – it adds a bit of colour)

1 tablespoon olive oil, for glazing

optional extras: nigella, sesame and poppy seeds

baking sheet, greased and lined with parchment paper

Makes 25–30 grissini

If you are using instant easy-blend/rapid-rise or fresh yeast, put all the ingredients in a big bowl. Mix with a wooden spoon and then your hands to form a dough.

If you are using dried/active dry yeast, put the flour in a big bowl and make a well in the middle. Sprinkle the yeast in the well and add half of the water. Cover and allow to rest for 15 minutes. Add the rest of the ingredients. Mix with a wooden spoon and then your hands to form a dough.

Stretch the dough out on a floured surface into a rectangle about 20 cm/8 in. wide and 1 cm/½ in. thick (and as long as it gets given the other dimensions). Glaze all over with the olive oil, cover and allow to rest for 1 hour.

Preheat the oven to 220°C (425°F) Gas 7.

Using a sharp knife, cut the dough in half lengthways. Cut 'fingers' of dough anywhere from 1–2 cm/½–¾ in. thick. Stretch each 'finger' as long and as thin as you want, and twist them too, if you like. Roll them in seeds, if using.

Lay the grissini on the prepared baking sheet. Bake in the preheated oven for 5–10 minutes, depending on the thickness of your grissini.

extra-long Hawaiian black salted breadsticks

These impressive breadsticks are always a popular canapé at parties – they go very well with drinks and dips, and are lovely just nibbled as they are.

450 g/3¾ cups plain/all-purpose flour

300 ml/1¼ cups warm water

3 tablespoons olive oil

1 tablespoon milk

9 g/1 tablespoon instant easy-blend/rapid-rise yeast

½ teaspoon brown sugar

60 ml/¼ cup olive oil, for brushing

110 g/½ cup black Hawaiian lava sea salt (or any other gourmet sea salt)

baking sheet, greased and lined with parchment paper

Makes about 24 breadsticks

To make the dough, put the flour in a food processor. In a measuring jug/cup mix together the warm water, olive oil, milk, yeast and brown sugar.

With the motor running, add the liquid to the flour in a steady stream. Process until all the liquid is incorporated and the dough forms a ball, about 3 minutes.

Turn out the dough onto a floured surface and knead for about 3 minutes, or until smooth. Form into a ball and put in an oiled bowl. Cover and leave to rise until doubled in volume.

Preheat the oven to 220°C (425°F) Gas 7.

Turn the dough out onto a floured surface. Roll into a rectangle, about 25 x 40 cm/10 x 16 in. in size, and 5mm/¼ in. thick. Use a sharp knife to cut 1-cm/½-in. strips of dough from the long side of the rectangle. Fold the strips in half and, with the palms of your hands, roll the dough into breadsticks 25 cm/10 in. long.

Arrange the breadsticks on the prepared baking sheet. Brush with olive oil and sprinkle with the black Hawaiian lava sea salt.

Bake in the preheated oven for 10 minutes, turn the sticks over, and bake for another 10 minutes, until golden. Set the sticks on a wire rack to cool.

From soft brioche to sticky pains aux raisins, breakfast is the perfect meal to experiment with enriched buns and loaves. Cinnamon, honey, nuts, saffron, raisins, butter and eggs are all used in this chapter to make delightful morning breads.

breakfast bakes

cinnamon raisin nut bread

Great for a fast, simple breakfast – on its own or toasted and buttered. Cinnamon, raisins and nuts are a classic combination.

650 g/5½ cups white strong/ bread flour

1½ tablespoons ground cinnamon

1 teaspoon salt

1 teaspoon light muscovado sugar

100 g/1 stick minus 1 tablespoon unsalted butter, chilled and diced

15 g/1 tablespoon fresh yeast

425 ml/1¾ cups milk, at room temperature

100 g/¾ cup (dark) raisins

75 g/scant ¾ cup walnut pieces, lightly toasted

large baking sheet, greased

Makes 1 large loaf

Sift the flour, cinnamon, salt and sugar into a large bowl. Rub in the butter with your fingertips until the mixture looks like fine breadcrumbs, then make a well in the centre. This is the dry mixture. Crumble the yeast into a bowl and whisk in the milk. This is the wet mixture. Pour the wet mixture into the well and mix in enough flour to make a thick batter. Cover the bowl and leave until thick and foamy – about 20 minutes.

Work in the rest of the flour from the edge of the bowl to make a soft but not sticky dough. Turn the dough out onto a floured surface. Knead for 10 minutes, until the dough is smooth and elastic. Place the dough back in the bowl, cover and leave for about 1½ hours, or until doubled in volume.

Turn the dough out onto a floured surface, and punch it down gently, to release the air. Add the (dark) raisins and nuts, and knead until thoroughly mixed. Shape the dough into an oval loaf about 25 x 15 cm/10 x 6 in. in size. Place the loaf on the prepared baking sheet, cover and leave to rise for about 45 minutes, or until doubled in size.

Preheated the oven to 220°C (425°F) Gas 7.

Place the loaf in the preheated oven and bake for 35 minutes, or until golden brown. Tap the bottom of the loaf – if it sounds hollow, it is done. Set the loaf on a wire rack to cool.

Well-flavoured but not over-sweet, this vibrant yellow loaf is wonderful spread with butter and fruit preserves, or toasted and served with ham and eggs.

saffron and honey bread

1 teaspoon saffron strands

500 g/4 cups white strong/bread flour, sifted

1 teaspoon salt

180 g/1½ sticks unsalted butter, chilled and diced

15 g/1 tablespoon fresh yeast

180 ml/¾ cup milk, lukewarm, plus extra, for brushing

2 tablespoons clear honey

900-g/2-lb/8½ x 4½-in. loaf tin/pan, greased

Makes 1 large loaf

Preheat the oven to 180°C (350°F) Gas 4.

Put the saffron in a heatproof ramekin dish and toast in the preheated oven for 10–15 minutes, until dark but not scorched. Allow to cool, then add 3 tablespoons water, cover and leave to soak overnight.

The next day, mix the flour and salt in a large bowl. Rub in the diced butter with your fingertips until the mixture looks like fine breadcrumbs. Make a well in the centre. This is the dry mixture. Crumble the yeast into a bowl, then whisk in the milk and honey to make a smooth liquid. This is the wet mixture. Pour the wet mixture into the well, followed by the saffron liquid. Mix with a wooden spoon and then your hands to form a dough.

Turn the dough out onto a floured surface. Knead for 10 minutes, until the dough is smooth and elastic. Place the dough back in the bowl, cover and leave for 1½ hours, or until doubled in volume.

Turn the dough out onto a floured surface, and punch it down gently, to release the air. Shape into a loaf to fit the tin/pan. Press the dough neatly into the prepared tin/pan. Cover and leave to rise for about 1 hour, or until doubled in volume.

Preheat the oven to 190°C (375°F) Gas 5.

Brush the risen loaf with milk, then bake in the preheated oven for 30 minutes, or until lightly browned. Reduce the temperature to 180°C (350°F) Gas 4 and bake for a further 15–20 minutes. Tap the bottom of the loaf – if it sounds hollow, it is done. Set the loaf on a wire rack to cool. It is best eaten within 4 days.

This bread has a lovely texture and is very nice toasted for breakfast. Rather than spreading it with butter, try it with zingy lemon curd or orange marmalade.

fig and hazelnut breakfast bread

500 g/4 cups strong bread flour

50 g/¼ cup caster/granulated sugar

2 teaspoons salt

7-g/¼-oz. packet instant easy-blend/rapid-rise yeast

2 tablespoons hazelnut oil

200 ml/¾ cup hand-hot water

2 tablespoons blanched hazelnuts, toasted and chopped

300 g/10 oz. ready-to-eat dried figs, quartered

Makes 2 loaves

Sift the flour, sugar and salt into a bowl and stir well. Add the yeast and stir again. Pour in the hazelnut oil and enough lukewarm water to bring the mixture together to a soft but not sticky dough. Add the hazelnuts and figs, and work them in.

Turn the dough out onto a floured surface. Knead for 10 minutes, until the dough is smooth and elastic. Divide into two rough loaves and put on oiled baking sheets spaced well apart. Leave for about 1 hour, or until doubled in volume.

Preheat the oven to 220°C (425°F) Gas 7.

Cut a couple of slashes in the top of each loaf and bake in the preheated oven for 25–30 minutes, or until golden brown. Tap the bottom of a loaf – if it sounds hollow, it is done. Set the loaves on a wire rack to cool.

brioche

This is a French classic. A good brioche is the perfect breakfast luxury. A subtly sweet bread enriched with egg and butter, it loves to be eaten with chocolate spread.

250 g/2 cups white strong/bread flour or French T55 flour

¾ teaspoon salt

2 tablespoons sugar

20 g/4 teaspoons fresh yeast or 9 g/1 tablespoon dried/active dry yeast

60 ml/¼ cup full-fat/whole milk, warmed slightly

2 eggs

100 g/6½ tablespoons soft butter

1 egg, beaten with a pinch of salt, for the egg wash

500-g/1-lb/6 x 4-in. loaf tin/pan, greased with butter

Makes 1 small loaf

In one mixing bowl, mix the flour, salt and sugar together and set aside. This is the dry mixture. In another mixing bowl, weigh out the yeast. Add the milk and stir until the yeast has dissolved. Lightly beat the eggs together, then add to the yeast solution. This is the wet mixture. Add the dry mixture to the wet mixture. Mix with a wooden spoon and then your hands to form a sticky dough.

Turn the dough out onto a floured surface. Knead for 10 minutes, until the dough is smooth and elastic. Pull small pieces off the butter and push into the dough. Knead the dough again to start incorporating the butter, and continue until all the butter has been incorporated. Cover, refrigerate and leave to rise for 1 hour, or until doubled in volume.

Turn the dough out onto a floured surface, and punch it down gently, to release the air. Divide the dough into 3 equal portions using a sharp, serrated knife. Take each portion of dough and roll between your hands until you get a perfectly round, smooth ball. Place the balls in the prepared loaf tin/pan. Cover and leave to rise for 30–45 minutes, or until slightly less than double the size.

Preheat the oven to 200°C (400°F) Gas 6. Place a roasting pan at the bottom of the oven. Fill a cup with water and set aside.

Brush the brioche all over with the egg wash. Snip the top of each bump on the brioche with kitchen scissors. Place the brioche in the preheated oven and pour the reserved cupful of water into the hot roasting pan. Bake for about 20 minutes, or until golden brown. Tap the bottom of the loaf – if it sounds hollow, it is done. Set the loaf on a wire rack to cool.

anadama bread

This bread has been eaten for years by fishermen on the Maritime coast of Canada and northeast coast of the USA.

500 g/4 cups white or wholemeal/whole-wheat strong/bread flour, or a mixture

2.5 g/1¼ teaspoons instant easy-blend/rapid-rise yeast, 5 g/1¾ teaspoons dried/active dry yeast, or 10 g/2 teaspoons fresh yeast

100 ml/scant ½ cup water

Cornmeal

200 ml/¾ cup plus 2 tablespoons boiling water

100 g/⅔ cup coarse ground yellow cornmeal/polenta

2 tablespoons lard or butter

2 teaspoons salt

100 g/6 tablespoons black treacle/molasses or honey

baking sheet, greased and lined with parchment paper

Makes 2 small loaves

For the cornmeal, mix the boiling water, cornmeal/polenta, lard, salt and black treacle/molasses in a bowl. Cover and soak overnight.

If you are using instant easy-blend/rapid-rise or fresh yeast, put all the ingredients in a big bowl, including the cornmeal mixture. Mix with a wooden spoon and then your hands to form a dough.

If you are using dried/active dry yeast, put the flour in a big bowl and make a well. Sprinkle the dry yeast in the well and add the water. Cover and allow to rest for 15 minutes. Add the rest of the ingredients, including the cornmeal mixture. Mix with a wooden spoon and then your hands to form a dough.

Turn the dough out onto a floured surface. Knead for 10 minutes – the dough will be quite sticky. Place the dough back in the bowl, cover and leave for about 1–2 hours, or until doubled in volume.

Turn the dough out onto a floured surface, and punch it down gently, to release the air. Divide the dough in half. Gently stretch each piece into a rectangle and then fold it up as you would a piece of paper to go into an envelope: fold the bottom edge two-thirds of the way up the rectangle and gently lay it down, then stretch the top edge away from the dough and fold it right over the top of the dough, placing it gently down. Transfer to the baking sheet. Flour the tops, cover with a dry kitchen towel, and leave to rest for 45 minutes, or until doubled in size.

Preheat the oven to 170°C (325°F) Gas 3.

Bake in the oven for 50–60 minutes. Tap the bottom of the loaf – if it sounds hollow, it is done. Set the loaf on a wire rack to cool.

These nutritious buns are portable, last for several days, and really fill you up. Great for breakfast on the run.

muesli stangen

300 g/2½ cups wholemeal/whole-wheat or spelt flour (or a mixture)

50 g/⅓ cup dark or light rye flour

1.5 g/¾ teaspoon instant easy-blend/rapid-rise yeast, 3 g/1 teaspoon dried/active dry yeast, or 6 g/1⅓ teaspoons fresh yeast

250 ml/1 cup water

1½ teaspoons salt

2–3 tablespoons black treacle/molasses, honey or maple syrup

muesli, to decorate

Soaked muesli

150 g/1¼ cups muesli of your choice (the sugar-free kind is best)

150 g/⅔ cup cold water

baking sheet, greased and lined with parchment paper

Makes 10 buns

Start by making the soaked muesli. Put the muesli in a little bowl, cover with the water and allow to soak for at least 1 hour before making the dough. You can leave it all day or overnight, if you like.

If you are using instant easy-blend/rapid-rise or fresh yeast, put all the ingredients, excluding the soaked muesli, into a big mixing bowl and bring them together into a big ball.

If you are using dried/active dry yeast, put the flour into a big mixing bowl and make a well. Sprinkle in the yeast and pour in half the water. Cover and allow to rest for 15 minutes. Add all the other ingredients, excluding the soaked muesli, and bring them together into a ball.

Turn the dough out onto a floured surface and knead for 10 minutes. It will be a sticky dough. Place the dough back in the bowl, cover and leave for 20 minutes.

Add the soaked muesli, squishing it into the dough thoroughly. Cover again and allow to rest for 2–3 hours.

Preheat the oven to 220°C (425°F) Gas 7.

Turn the sticky dough out onto a floured surface, and divide it into 10 equal portions. Roll each portion into a tight ball. Fill a plate with muesli. Roll each ball of dough around on the plate, stretching it into a sausage about 10 cm/4 in. long. Place on the prepared baking sheet, leaving space between each bun.

Flatten the buns slightly , then brush liberally with water. Bake in the preheated oven for 20 minutes, or until golden. Tap the bottom of a bun – if it sounds hollow, it is done. Set on a wire rack to cool.

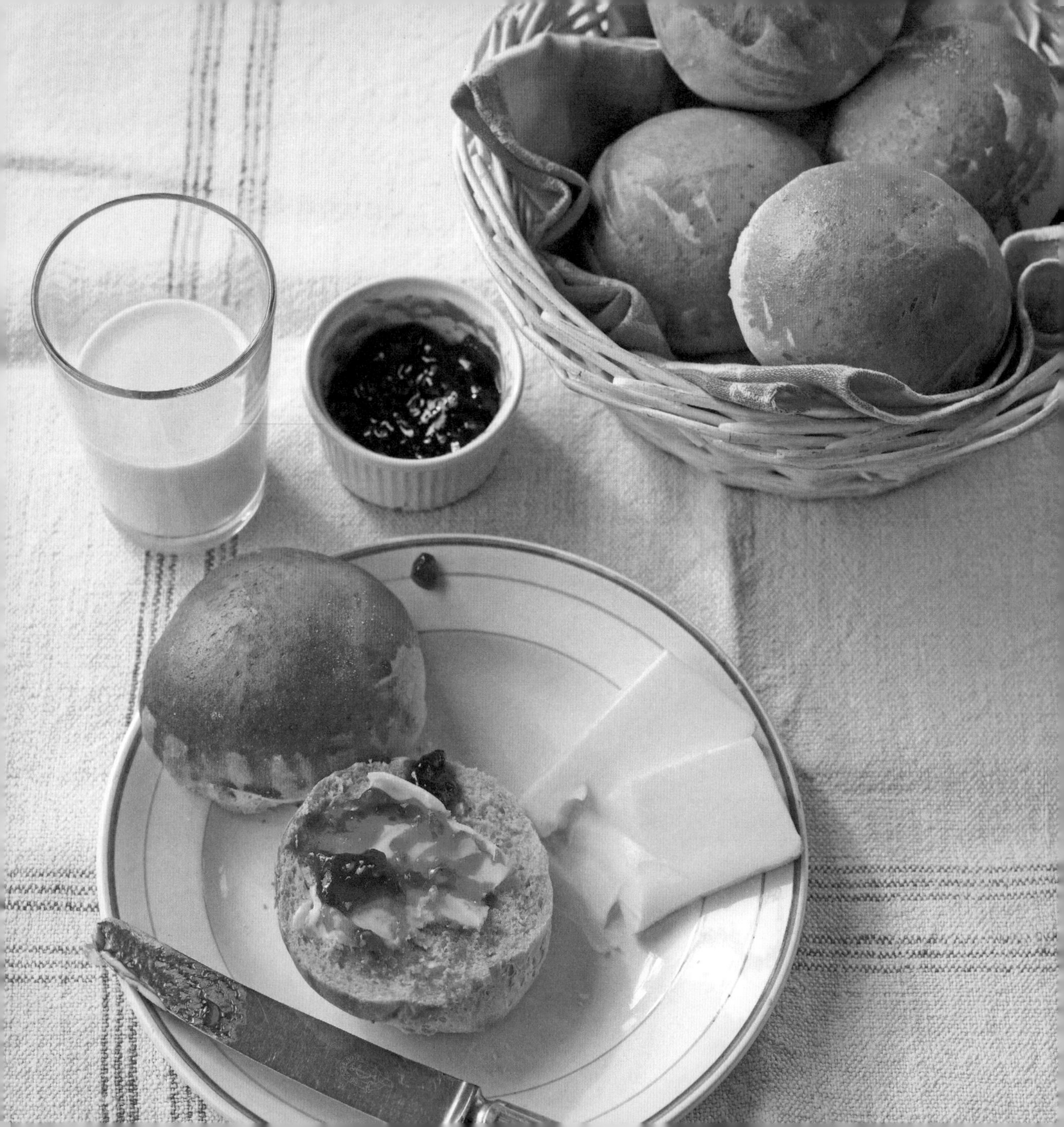

Milk bread or morning bread has long been eaten all over the world. It was a way of using up milk and a way of getting the valuable protein and vitamins from milk into the diet in a more portable way! Milk bread is delicious and the crumb and crust are soft and chewy. Eat with butter and jam.

milk bread

300 g/2½ cups white strong/bread, plain/all-purpose or wholemeal/whole-wheat flour (or a mixture)

1.5 g/¾ teaspoon instant easy-blend/rapid-rise yeast, 3 g/1 teaspoon dried/active dry yeast, or 6 g/1⅓ teaspoons fresh yeast

200 ml/¾ cup plus 2 tablespoons full-fat/whole milk, heated up to boiling point, then cooled to room temperature

1½ teaspoons salt

Glaze

1 tablespoon clear honey

1 tablespoon milk

baking sheet, greased and lined with parchment paper

Makes 8 buns

If you are using instant easy-blend/rapid-rise or fresh yeast, put all the ingredients in a big bowl. Mix with a wooden spoon and then your hands to form a dough.

If you are using dried/active dry yeast, put the flour in a big bowl and make a well. Sprinkle the dry yeast in the well and add half the milk. Cover and allow to rest for 15 minutes. Add the rest of the ingredients. Mix with a wooden spoon and then your hands to form a dough.

Turn the dough out onto a floured surface. Knead for 10 minutes, until the dough is smooth and elastic. Place the dough back in the bowl, cover and leave for 1–2 hours, or until doubled in volume.

Turn the dough out onto a floured surface, and punch it down gently, to release the air. Divide the dough into 8 equal portions and form into tight balls. Place them on a floured kitchen towel, cover and allow to rest for 45 minutes. In the meantime, heat the honey and milk together for the glaze, then allow to cool down.

Preheat the oven to 220°C (425°F) Gas 7.

Transfer the buns to the prepared baking sheet and brush with the milk and honey glaze. Bake the buns in the preheated oven for 15–20 minutes, until golden brown. Tap the bottom of a bun – if it sounds hollow, it is done. Set the buns on a wire rack to cool.

seedy loaf

100 g/scant 1 cup wheat germ, or wheat germ and wheat bran mix

100 g/1¼ cups wheat flakes

100 g/scant 1 cup walnut pieces

50 g/6 tablespoons sunflower seeds

50 g/6 tablespoons pumpkin seeds

50 g/6 tablespoons sesame seeds

50 g/6 tablespoons linseeds

250 g/1½ cups bulgur wheat or cracked wheat

1 teaspoon bicarbonate of soda/baking soda

1 teaspoon salt

1 large/US extra large egg

2 tablespoons clear honey

500 ml/2¼ cups natural/plain yogurt (not fat-free)

a 900-g/2-lb/8½ x 4½-in. loaf tin/pan, greased and lined with parchment paper

Makes 1 large loaf

This German recipe makes a loaf that looks more like a mosaic of seeds, nuts and grains than bread. It is dense and very nutritious, good with butter and honey, soft cheeses and salads. It is also very adaptable – the wheat flakes can be replaced with rye flakes, the walnuts with chopped almonds, cashews or toasted pine nuts.

Put the wheat germ and flakes, walnuts, seeds, bulghur wheat, bicarbonate of soda/baking soda and salt into a large bowl. Stir with a wooden spoon until thoroughly combined. This is the dry mixture.

In a small bowl, beat the egg with the honey and yoghurt. This is the wet mixture. Stir the wet mixture into the dry mixture, then leave to soak for 30 minutes.

Preheat the oven to 180°C (350°F) Gas 4.

Stir the bread mixture thoroughly, then scrape into the prepared tin/pan and spread evenly. Bake for 30 minutes then cover loosely with foil or parchment paper to prevent over-browning and cook for 25 minutes more. Test the loaf is cooked by pushing a skewer into the centre – if it comes out clean the loaf is ready. If the skewer comes out sticky with dough, cook for a further 5 minutes and test again.

Carefully turn out onto a wire rack, remove the parchment paper and leave to cool completely before slicing. Wrap well and eat within 2 days, or toast. Not suitable for freezing.

croissants

Once you have mastered the method for making croissants, you can recreate your own little French café and bake *pains aux raisins*, too (see page 125).

250 g/2 cups white strong/bread flour

1½ tablespoons caster/granulated sugar

1 teaspoon salt

10 g/2 teaspoons fresh yeast or 5 g/1½ teaspoons dried/active dry yeast

125 ml/½ cup warm water

150 g/10 tablespoons butter, slightly soft

1 egg, beaten with a pinch of salt, for the egg wash

baking sheet, greased and lined with parchment paper

Makes 8 croissants

In one mixing bowl, mix the flour, sugar and salt together. This is the dry mixture. In another mixing bowl, dissolve the yeast in the water. This is the wet mixture. Add the dry mixture to the wet mixture. Mix with a wooden spoon and then your hands to form a dough.

Turn the dough out onto a floured surface. Knead for 10 minutes, until the dough is smooth and elastic. Place the dough back in the bowl, cover and leave to rest in the refrigerator overnight. If you are using dried/active dry yeast, leave the dough to rise for another 30 minutes at room temperature before putting it into the refrigerator overnight. This will give the yeast a kick-start.

Turn the dough out onto a floured surface, and punch it down gently, to release the air. Pull the dough outwards from the edges until you have a rough square about 12 cm/5 in. in size. Cut the butter to achieve a rectangle roughly half the size of your square of dough. Make sure the dough is about the same thickness as the rectangle of butter.

Place the butter diagonally across the middle of the square of dough. Fold the corners of the dough towards the middle so that they envelop the butter and you get a neat package. Stretch the dough if necessary to completely encase the butter. Press down on the dough using a rolling pin to distribute the butter evenly through it inside the envelope.

Start rolling the dough lengthwise until you have a long rectangle about 1 cm/½ in. thick. Fold the bottom third of the rectangle over. Fold the top third over. You should now have 3 rectangular pieces of dough piled on top of each other; this is your first turn.

Make a small indentation into the dough with your fingertip to remind you that you have made one turn. Wrap the dough in clingfilm/plastic wrap and refrigerate for 20 minutes.

Remove the dough from the refrigerator and repeat this process twice. You will now have given the pastry 3 turns and should have 3 indentations. Wrap the dough in clingfilm/plastic wrap and refrigerate for 40 minutes.

Remove the dough from the refrigerator and roll it out to a rectangle about 24 x 38 cm/ 10 x 15 in. in size. Cut the rectangle into 8 long, thin triangles. Starting from the shortest side, roll up each triangle into a croissant. Place the croissants on the prepared baking sheets, allowing a little space between them so that they have room to rise. Leave to rise until you see the folds in the pastry separating.

Preheat the oven to 240°C (475°F) Gas 9. Place a roasting pan at the bottom of the oven. Fill a cup with water.

When the croissants are ready to be baked, brush them lightly all over with the egg wash. Place the baking sheets in the preheated oven, pour the reserved cupful of water onto the hot roasting pan and lower the oven temperature to 220°C (425°F) Gas 7. Bake for 15–20 minutes, or until golden brown.

Don't worry if you see butter seeping out of the croissants during baking – it should all be absorbed when the croissants cool. Let the croissants cool slightly on wire racks before eating, then serve slightly warm.

These pains aux raisins are really impressive if you have guests staying for the weekend.

pains aux raisins

1 quantity Croissant dough
(see page 122 – follow the recipe
to the point where the dough has
been rolled out and turned 3 times,
and chilled for 40 minutes)

150 g/1 cup (dark) raisins

smooth apricot jam, warmed in a
pan, for glazing

icing/confectioners' sugar, for
glazing (optional)

Custard

20 g/2½ tablespoons white plain/
all-purpose flour

10 g/4 teaspoons cornflour/
cornstarch

250 ml/1 cup whole milk

1 large/US extra large egg,
lightly beaten

50 g/¼ cup sugar

1 teaspoon vanilla extract

*2 baking sheets, greased and
lined with parchment paper*

Makes about 19 pains aux raisins

For the custard, whisk the flour and cornflour/cornstarch with one-quarter of the milk, until smooth. Add the egg. In a saucepan, put the remaining milk, sugar and vanilla extract, and heat until the mixture comes to a boil. Add the flour mixture and whisk. Keep whisking over the heat until it starts to thicken, then cook for 2 minutes more. Transfer the custard to a bowl. Place clingfilm/plastic wrap on top of the custard to prevent a skin from forming. Allow to cool and refrigerate for up to 24 hours, until needed.

Remove the croissant dough from the refrigerator and roll out to a rectangle about 24 x 38 cm/10 x 15 in. in size. Spread the custard on the dough, and sprinkle the raisins over the top. Now roll up the dough from a longer side to make a long log. Wrap the log in clingfilm/plastic wrap and refrigerate for 30 minutes.

Discard the clingfilm/plastic wrap and cut the dough into 2-cm/¾-in. slices. You will get about 19 slices. Place on the baking sheets, tucking the end of each swirl underneath to help it retain its shape during baking. Allow space between them. Leave to rise until you see the folds in the pastry separating.

Preheat the oven to 240°C (475°F) Gas 9. Place a roasting pan at the bottom of the oven. Fill a cup with water.

Place the baking sheets in the preheated oven, pour the reserved cupful of water onto the hot roasting pan and lower the oven temperature to 220°C (425°F) Gas 7. Bake for 12–15 minutes, or until golden. Brush the warm jam over each warm pastry.

To make an icing, mix a few tablespoons of icing/confectioners' sugar with a little cold water, until smooth and runny. When the pastries are cold, drizzle the icing over them.

Bread doesn't have to be savoury. This chapter brings together some of the world's favourite sweet doughs, with plenty of family classics, from iced buns to apple buns, and a selection of festive treats such as hot cross buns, tsoureki and stollen.

buns and sweet breads

10 g/2 teaspoons fresh yeast or 5 g/1½ teaspoons dried/active dry yeast

3 tablespoons sugar

200 ml/¾ cup warm water

200 g/1⅔ cups plain/all-purpose flour

150 g/1 cup sultanas/golden raisins

150 g/1 cup (Zante) currants

1 teaspoon ground ginger

1 teaspoon ground cinnamon

¼ teaspoon ground cloves

grated zest of 2 oranges and 3 lemons

200 g/1⅔ cups white strong/bread flour

½ teaspoon salt

90 g/6 tablespoons soft butter

1 large/US extra large egg, beaten

Crosses

3 tablespoons vegetable oil

75 g/⅔ cup plain/all-purpose flour

½ teaspoon salt

Glaze

150 g/¾ cup sugar

½ orange, cut in 4, and ½ lemon, cut in 2

2 cinnamon sticks, 5 cloves and 3 star anise

baking sheet, lined with parchment paper

piping bag fitted with a small round nozzle/tip

Makes 15

hot cross buns

This is the traditional Easter treat in the UK. Start making these buns long before Easter if you like, because there's no reason they can't be enjoyed all year round. They taste great toasted and dripping with melted butter.

Make the mixture for the crosses. Mix the oil with 90 ml/⅓ cup water. In a small bowl, mix the flour and salt together. Add the oil mixture to the flour mixture, and stir to a smooth paste. Cover and set aside.

Next, make the glaze. Put all the ingredients in a saucepan with 250 ml/1 cup water, and bring to a boil. When it comes to a boil, take off the heat and set aside to infuse.

In a mixing bowl, weigh out the yeast. Add the sugar and water, and stir until the yeast and sugar have dissolved. Add the plain/all-purpose flour and stir until well mixed. This is the pre-ferment. Cover the bowl and leave for 30 minutes, or until doubled in size.

Meanwhile, mix the dried fruit, spices and zest together, and set aside.

In another mixing bowl, mix the strong/bread flour and salt. This is the dry mixture. Pull small pieces off the butter and lightly rub into the dry mixture using your fingertips.

After 30 minutes, the pre-ferment will have risen. Add the egg and pre-ferment to the flour mixture, and bring it together with your hands to form a dough.

Turn the dough out onto a floured surface. Knead for 10 minutes, until the dough is smooth and elastic. Place back in the bowl, cover and leave for 30 minutes. (You can refrigerate the dough and continue the recipe the next day, if necessary. In this case, leave the dough at room temperature for 15 minutes before continuing.)

Lightly dust a clean work surface with flour. Transfer the dough to the floured work surface.

Divide the dough into 15 equal portions using a metal dough scraper or sharp, serrated knife. Each portion should weigh about 70 g/2½ oz. If you want to be as accurate as possible, weigh each piece and add or subtract dough from the portions until they all weigh the same.

Take one portion of dough and roll between your hands until you get a perfectly round ball. Put the ball on the prepared baking sheet, and repeat with the remaining dough. Allow a little space between them so that they have room to rise and arrange them in neat rows and lines. Cover the balls and leave to rise until about double the size.

Preheat the oven to 220°C (425°F) Gas 7. Place a roasting pan at the bottom of the oven to preheat. Fill a cup with water and set aside.

Fill a piping bag with the reserved mixture for the crosses. Pipe continuous lines across the tops of the buns in both directions.

Place the baking sheet in the preheated oven, pour the reserved cupful of water onto the hot roasting pan and lower the oven temperature to 180°C (350°F) Gas 4. Bake for about 10–15 minutes, or until golden brown.

Remove the buns from the oven. Brush lightly with the cold, reserved glaze. Allow to cool on the tray and serve.

500 g/5 cups plain/all-purpose flour

75 g/6 tablespoons sugar

2.5 g/1¼ teaspoons instant easy-blend/rapid-rise yeast, 5 g/1¾ teaspoons dried/active dry yeast, or 10 g/2 teaspoons fresh yeast

300 g/1¼ cups milk, heated up to just below boiling point, then cooled to room temperature

2½ teaspoons salt

1 egg

75 g/5 tablespoons butter

Decoration

225 g/2¼ cups icing/confectioners' sugar

hundreds and thousands/sprinkles, coloured rock sugar or glacé/candied cherries, cut into small bits, to sprinkle (optional)

2 baking sheets, greased and lined with parchment paper

Makes 12 buns

These are classic English buns that you can find in any good, traditional bakery. They are easy to make and shape, are rather plain and have a thick coating of shiny, white icing on the top. They are great buns to make with children.

iced buns

Put the flour into a big mixing bowl and make a well. Add the sugar and yeast to the well and pour in the milk. Close the well by flicking some flour over the surface of the milk, then cover and allow to rest for 1 hour.

Sprinkle the salt around the edge of the flour and add the egg. Mix with a wooden spoon and then your hands to form a dough.

Turn the dough out onto a floured surface. Knead for 10 minutes, until the dough is smooth and elastic. Add the butter and knead for another 10 minutes. Put the dough back into the bowl and cover. Allow to rest for 2 hours.

Turn the dough out onto a floured surface, and punch it down gently, to release the air. Divide the dough into 12 equal portions and shape each portion into a tight ball. Cover and leave to rest for 15 minutes.

Rock each ball back and forth to elongate them into sausages and place them on the prepared baking sheets. Cover the buns with a dry tea towel/kitchen towel and allow to rest for 1 hour.

Preheat the oven to 220°C (425°F) Gas 7.

Bake the buns in the preheated oven for 20 minutes, or until golden. Set on a wire rack to cool.

Mix the icing/confectioners' sugar with 2 tablespoons water. When the buns are cool, ice them, and decorate with sprinkles, if using.

300 g/2½ cups plain/all-purpose flour

1.5 g/¾ teaspoon instant easy-blend/rapid-rise yeast, 3 g/1 teaspoon dried/active dry yeast, or 6 g/2 teaspoons fresh yeast

50 g/¼ cup sugar

200 ml/¾ cup milk, heated up to just below boiling point, then cooled to room temperature

1½ teaspoons salt

50 g/3 tablespoons butter

Filling

75 g/½ cup dried fruit, such as (dark) raisins, sultanas/golden raisins or Zante currants, or a mixture

25 g/2½ tablespoons dried mixed peel, chopped

50 g/¼ cup soft light brown or demerara/raw sugar

2 tablespoons melted butter, cooled

Glaze

2 big spoonfuls of clear honey, melted

2 baking sheets, greased and lined with parchment paper

Makes 8–12 buns

This is another favourite sweet bread recipe in the UK. Enjoy these delicious sticky buns with a cup of strong tea for a truly English experience!

Chelsea buns

Put the flour into a big bowl and make a well. Sprinkle the yeast and sugar into the well and pour over the milk. Flick some flour over the surface of the milk to close the well, cover and allow to rest for 1 hour.

Add the salt, mix with a wooden spoon and then your hands to form a dough.

Turn the dough out onto a floured surface. Knead for 10 minutes, until the dough is smooth and elastic. Add the butter and knead for another 10 minutes. Put the dough back into the bowl and cover. Allow to rest for 2 hours.

Meanwhile, mix the dried fruit, peel and sugar for the filling.

Turn the dough out onto a floured surface, and punch it down gently, to release the air.

Roll the dough into a rectangle about 30 x 23 cm/12 x 9 in. in size. Brush it with the cooled melted butter and sprinkle the sugar and fruit mixture evenly on top to coat it. Roll the dough up, tugging it gently towards you at each roll to achieve a tight sausage. Cut the sausage into 8–12 slices. Place the slices on the prepared baking sheets and lightly flour the tops. Cover with a tea towel/kitchen towel and allow to rest for 1 hour.

Preheat the oven to 220°C (425°F) Gas 7.

Bake the buns in the preheated oven for 15 minutes, until golden brown. Remove from the oven and brush with melted honey while they are still hot. Set on a wire rack to cool.

maple syrup buns

Maple syrup is a traditional sweetener in eastern Canada and the northeastern United States. As it is completely unrefined, it retains many of its natural nutrients.

500 g/4 cups plain/all-purpose flour

2.5 g/1 ¼ teaspoons instant easy-blend/rapid-rise yeast, 5 g/1¾ teaspoons dried/active dry yeast, or 10 g/2 teaspoons fresh yeast

2 tablespoons maple sugar (or brown sugar if you cannot get maple sugar)

250 ml/1 cup milk, heated up to boiling point, then cooled to room temperature

2 eggs, lightly beaten

2 medium potatoes, peeled, boiled, mashed and cooled

2½ teaspoons salt

1 tablespoon ground cinnamon

2 tablespoons lard or butter

125 ml/½ cup maple syrup, to glaze

round cookie cutter (optional)

2 baking sheets, greased and lined with parchment paper

sugar thermometer

Makes 4 dozen buns

Put the flour in a bowl and make a well. Add the yeast and sugar to the well and pour in the milk. Flick some flour on the milk to close the well. Cover and allow to rest for 1 hour.

Stir the eggs into the mashed potatoes. Mix in the salt, cinnamon and lard or butter. Add the potato mixture to flour mixture. Mix with a wooden spoon and then your hands to form a dough.

Turn the dough out onto a floured surface. Knead for 10 minutes, until the dough is smooth and elastic. It will be sticky. Place the dough back in the bowl, cover and leave for about 2 hours, or until doubled in volume.

Turn the dough out onto a floured surface, and punch it down gently, to release the air. Roll the dough out until 2.5 cm/1 in. thick. Cut it into squares with a knife or use a cookie cutter to stamp out rounds about 5 cm/2 in. across. Place them on the prepared baking sheets, lightly flour the tops and cover with a dry tea towel/kitchen towel. Allow to rest for 1 hour.

Preheat the oven to 220°C (425°F) Gas 7.

Bake the buns in the preheated oven for 15–20 minutes, or until golden brown. Set on a wire rack to cool slightly.

Pour the maple syrup into a saucepan and boil until it reaches the 'thread' stage – 112°C/234°F on a sugar thermometer. Drizzle it onto the buns while they are still warm.

475 g/3¾ cups plain/all-purpose flour

50 g/¼ cup sugar

2.5 g/1¼ teaspoons instant easy-blend/rapid-rise yeast, 5 g/1¾ teaspoons dried/active dry yeast, or 10 g/2 teaspoons fresh yeast

3 tablespoons milk, heated to boiling point, then cooled

150 ml/scant ⅔ cup water

2½ teaspoons salt

1 egg

50 g/3 tablespoons butter

Predough

25 g/3 tablespoons plain/all-purpose flour

Filling

3–4 apples, peeled, cored and cut into small pieces

50 g/¼ cup brown sugar

½ teaspoon ground cinnamon

pinch each of ground cloves, nutmeg and salt

grated zest of 1 lemon

50 g/3 tablespoons butter

Glaze

1 egg

pinch of salt

pinch of sugar

Decoration

ground cinnamon, to sprinkle

2 baking sheets, greased and lined with parchment paper

Makes 16 buns

apple buns

The great thing about apples is that you can more or less get them all year round, so you can make these buns any time.

To make the predough, mix the flour with 125 ml/½ cup water. Cover with clingfilm/plastic wrap and leave to rest for 12–24 hours.

Place all the filling ingredients into a saucepan and simmer gently until the apples are soft. Add a little water if the apples stick. Remove from the heat, cover and set aside until you need it.

For the dough, put the flour into the bowl and make a well. Sprinkle the sugar and yeast into the well and pour over the milk and water. Close the well by flicking some flour over the surface of the liquid. Cover and allow to rest for 1 hour.

Sprinkle the salt around the edge of the flour, and add the egg and predough. Mix with your hands to form a dough.

Turn the dough out onto a floured surface. Knead for 10 minutes, then add the butter and knead for another 10 minutes. Place the dough back in the bowl, cover and leave for 2 hours.

Turn the dough out onto a floured surface, and punch it down gently, to release the air. Shape the dough into a tight sausage. Divide the sausage into 16 portions, cover and leave for 15 minutes.

Take a piece of dough and stretch it gently with your hands into a disc 5 mm/¼ in. thick. Put a spoonful of the apple mixture in the centre of the disc and pull the edges up around it. Press to seal, and place seam-side down on a prepared baking sheet. Repeat with the remaining dough. Cover and leave to rest for 45 minutes.

Preheat the oven to 220°C (425°F) Gas 7. Beat the glaze ingredients together with a tablespoon of water.

Glaze the buns and sprinkle with ground cinnamon, then bake in the preheated oven for 15 minutes. Set on a wire rack to cool.

Tsoureki is a beautiful sweet bread used to break the fast at Eastertime in Greece, and is lovely for celebrations.

tsoureki

40 g/2½ tablespoons fresh yeast or 20 g/2 tablespoons dried/active dry yeast

50 ml/¼ cup warm water

240 g/2 cups white strong/bread flour

30 g/2 tablespoons unsalted butter (plus a pinch of salt) or salted butter

80 g/⅓ cup sugar

grated zest of ½ orange

1 teaspoon ground mahlepi/mahleb (ground black cherry pits)

1 teaspoon ground cardamom

1 egg

1 egg, beaten with a pinch of salt, for the egg wash

baking sheet, greased and lined with parchment paper

Makes 1 small loaf

In a mixing bowl, weigh out the yeast. Add the water and stir until the yeast has dissolved. Add 40 g/⅓ cup of the flour and mix with a wooden spoon. This is the pre-ferment. Cover and leave for 30 minutes, or until doubled in volume.

Meanwhile, melt the butter in a saucepan. Add the sugar to the melted butter and turn down the heat to low. Stir until the sugar has dissolved, then take the pan off the heat and mix in the zest and spices. Leave to cool until just slightly warm, whisking from time to time. Whisk the egg into the warm butter mixture.

Add the remaining 200 g/1⅔ cups flour and the butter mixture to the pre-ferment, and mix to a stiff dough.

Turn the dough out onto a floured surface. Knead for 10 minutes, until the dough is smooth and elastic. Place the dough back in the bowl, cover and leave for about 1 hour, or until doubled in volume.

Turn the dough out onto a floured surface, and punch it down gently, to release the air. Divide the dough into 4 equal portions. Roll each piece into a sausage, 25 cm/10 in. long, tapered at the end. Press the ends together, then plait/braid the dough, tucking the ends in. Place on the baking sheet, cover and leave to rise for 30–45 minutes, or until slightly less than double the size.

Preheat the oven to 240°C (475°F) Gas 9. Place a roasting pan at the bottom of the oven. Fill a cup with water and set aside.

Brush the tsoureki with the egg wash, place in the preheated oven, pour the reserved cupful of water onto the hot roasting pan and lower the oven temperature to 200°C (400°F) Gas 6. Bake for about 20 minutes, or until golden brown. Tap the bottom of the loaf – if it sounds hollow, it is done. Set the loaf on a wire rack to cool.

marzipan stollen

Stollen is eaten at Christmastime in Germany. It contains a delicious marzipan centre and plenty of dried fruit. Make the dried fruit mixture a week in advance.

10 g/2 teaspoons fresh yeast or 5 g/1½ teaspoons dried/active dry yeast

20 ml/4 teaspoons milk, warmed

20 g/2½ tablespoons white strong/bread flour

50 g/3 tablespoons plus 1 teaspoon soft butter

2 tablespoons sugar

¼ teaspoon salt

¼ teaspoon ground cardamom

¼ teaspoon vanilla extract

1 egg, beaten

150 g/1¼ cups white strong/bread flour

150 g/1 stick plus 2 tablespoons butter

100 g/3½ oz. marzipan

vanilla sugar, to taste

icing/confectioners' sugar, for dusting

Fruit mixture

60 g/½ cup sultanas/golden raisins

15 g/2 tablespoons toasted flaked/slivered almonds

15 g/1 generous tablespoon diced candied citrus peel

freshly squeezed juice and grated zest of 1 orange and 1 lemon

1 tablespoon rum

Glaze

30 g/¼ cup smooth apricot jam

45 g/3 tablespoons butter

2 tablespoons sugar

1 tablespoon milk

baking sheet, greased and lined with parchment paper

Makes 1 medium stollen

In a mixing bowl, mix together all the ingredients for the fruit mixture. Cover with clingfilm/plastic wrap and leave in a cool place for 1 week, until most of the liquid has been absorbed.

To make the dough, weigh out the yeast in a mixing bowl. Add the milk and stir until the yeast has dissolved. Add the 20 g/2½ tablespoons flour and mix with a wooden spoon. This is the pre-ferment. Cover and leave for 30 minutes, or until doubled in volume.

In another mixing bowl, beat the 50 g/3 tablespoons plus 1 teaspoon butter, sugar, salt, cardamom and vanilla extract until soft. Add the egg, little by little, whisking well.

Mix 1 tablespoon of the flour (from the 150 g/1¼ cups) into the fruit mixture to absorb any surplus moisture. Set aside.

When the pre-ferment has risen, stir it into the butter mixture. Add the remaining 150 g/1¼ cups flour to the mixture and mix until it comes together. Cover and leave to stand for 10 minutes.

Turn the dough out onto a floured surface. Knead for 10 minutes, until the dough is smooth and elastic. Add the reserved dried fruit mixture to the dough and knead gently until thoroughly mixed in. Place the dough back in the bowl, cover and leave for about 1 hour, or until doubled in volume

Turn the dough out onto a floured surface, and punch it down gently, to release the air. Shape the dough into a ball and leave for 5 minutes, until it is workable. Meanwhile, shape the marzipan into a short sausage.

Dust the dough with a little flour so that it does not stick to the rolling pin. Roll out the dough to a rough square. Place the marzipan sausage in the middle. Pull the dough over the ends of the marzipan. Fold the side closest to you over the marzipan to enclose it completely. Fold the side furthest from you over. Roll the stollen over so that the seam is underneath. Use both hands to mould the dough around the marzipan.

Transfer the stollen to the prepared baking sheet, cover and leave to rise in a warm place for 30 minutes, or until slightly less than double the size.

Preheat the oven to 200°C (400°F) Gas 6. Place a roasting pan at the bottom of the oven to preheat. Fill a cup with water and set aside.

Place the baking sheet in the preheated oven, pour the reserved cupful of water into the hot roasting pan and lower the oven temperature to 180°C (350°F) Gas 4. Bake the stollen for about 20 minutes, or until golden. Tap the bottom of the stollen – if it sounds hollow, it is done. Set the stollen on a wire rack to cool slightly.

Dislodge any darkened raisins stuck to the baking sheet with a sharp knife, but take care not to damage the stollen.

Melt the 150 g/1 stick plus 2 tablespoons butter, and brush over the stollen. Allow to seep into the dough, then repeat twice more. Leave to cool completely.

Put the ingredients for the glaze in a pan and bring to a boil. Brush the glaze all over (top and bottom) the cold stollen.

Generously dust a tray with vanilla sugar and put the freshly glazed stollen on it. Dust the top and sides with the vanilla sugar, too. Finally, dust the stollen with icing/confectioners' sugar.

index

picture credits

Martin Brigdale
Pages 1, 2, 4, 46, 65 insert

Peter Cassidy
Pages 3, 10 all inserts, 21, 30, 31, 33, 36, 42, 49, 53, 56, 67, 80, 83, 88, 96, 99, 100, 114, 117, 118, 126, 130, 133, 134, 137

Vanessa Davies
Page 22

Georgia Glynn-Smith
Page 68

Jonathan Gregson
Page 103

William Lingwood
Page 76

Steve Painter
Pages 5, 6, 8 insert, 9, 11, 12, 14, 25, 26, 34, 35 insert, 37, 38, 45, 57, 59 insert, 60, 64, 72, 73 insert, 75, 79, 84, 94 insert, 95, 104, 105, 113, 123 insert, 124, 127, 129, 138, 141 insert, 144

William Reavell
Pages 7, 13, 16-19, 29, 55, 62, 63, 66, 77, 78, 90-93, 108, 110, 142-143

Philip Webb
Pages 41, 50, 106, 109

Kate Whitaker
Pages 51, 54, 71, 87, 120, 121, endpapers

Francesca Yorke
Page 86 insert

recipe credits

Emmanuel Hadjiandreou
Armenian Flatbreads
Bagels
Baguettes
Bread Rolls
Brioche
Challah
Ciabatta
Cracked Pepper Naan
Croissants
Dark Rye Bread
Focaccia
Hot Cross Buns
Marzipan Stollen
Olive and Herb Bread
Pains aux Raisins
Pita Breads
Pizza Dough
Tsoureki
White Sourdough
Wholegrain Sourdough

Jane Mason
Anadama Bread
Apple Buns
Beer Bread
Chelsea Buns
Cornmeal Buns
Grissini
Iced Buns
Maple Syrup Buns
Milk Bread
Muesli Stangan
Olive Oil Rolls
Roti or Chapati
Simple White Bread
Swedish Cracker Bread

Linda Collister
Ciabatta Rolls
Cinnamon Raisin Nut Bread
Cottage Cheese Rolls
Little Spring Onion Breads
Oat Baps
Saffron and Honey Bread
Seedy Loaf
The Grant Loaf
Tuscan Fresh Sage and Olive Oil Bread

Miisa Mink
Barley Flatbreads
Rye Baguettes
Rye Crispbreads
Rye Pockets

Dunja Gulin
Simple Gluten-free Loaf
Soft-shell Tacos

Chloe Coker and Jane Montgomery
Simple Soda Bread
Tomato and Pesto Bread

Maxine Clark
Parmesan Soda Bread

Hannah Miles
Gluten-free Flatbreads
Gluten-free Soda Bread

Valerie Aikman-Smith
Extra-long Hawaiian Black Salted Breadsticks

Tori Finch
Mediterranean Bread

Brian Glover
Courgette and Ricotta Loaf

Liz Franklin
Fig and Hazelnut Breakfast Bread

Ross Dobson
Four Flour Bread